Land Where the Trees Talk and Other Plays

South Asian Canadian Literature Series

General Editor: Uma Parameswaran

SACLIT 1	**Trishanku and Other Writings** Uma Parameswaran
SACLIT 2	**Sons Must Die and Other Plays** Uma Parameswaran
SACLIT 3	**Five or Six Characters in Search of Toronto and Other Plays** Rana Bose
SACLIT 4	**Land Where the Trees Talk and Other Plays** Rahul Varma

Land Where the Trees Talk and Other Plays

RAHUL VARMA

Selected and with an Introduction
by

Uma Parameswaran

PRESTIGE

Published by
Prestige Books
3/28, East Patel Nagar
New Delhi 110 008

1998

ISBN: 81-7551-022-6

Photo Typesetting by
Pivot Computers
Delhi 110 006
Ph. 2934490

Printed at
Chaman Offset Printers
New Delhi 110 002

Contents

Introduction
Rahul Varma and *Teesri Duniya*

UMA PARAMESWARAN

"I am determined to write issue-oriented, provocative, socio-political plays which are inspired by and have emerged from the grass roots of our society," says Rahul Varma of *Teesri Duniya*, a Montreal-based theatre company. This determination is evident in all his efforts. Author of ten plays, some of which have been co-authored by others, Varma and *Teesri Duniya*, of which he is a founding member, have gained recognition in Montreal, though they are little known elsewhere in the country. While *Teesri Duniya*, and *Serai*, also of Montreal, continue to be the leaders in scripts and staging, and *TSAR* (*Toronto South Asian Review*, now renamed without as handy an acronym) continues to be the leading periodical, the number of theatre and literary forums started by South Asian Canadians has been steadily increasing. In Vancouver, *Sath* (a theatre group in which Sadhu Binning is a leading playwright), *Ankur* (a periodical) and *Rungh* (a glossy periodical that features interviews and review articles on both, the Indian sub continent and the diaspora) have been making waves. In Toronto, *Cahoots Theatre* has been working on several plays, and no doubt we will soon be hearing more from their playwrights—Dilara Ally, Sheila James and Sonia Dhillon

Though South Asian Canadian literature has established its identity, critical paradigms and strategies have not yet been worked out. We have to coin the terminology and frameworks that can not only showcase but also promote cross cultural understanding. Both *Serai* and *Teesri Duniya* see themselves as cross-cultural or inter-cultural theatre groups, and have active members from at least half a dozen different ethnocentric origins. However, since the founding members are South Asians, I give them a South Asian Canadian identity.

South Asian Canadian theatre came of age in the 1980s and one hopes the 1990s will establish a national networking of the various theatre groups so that at least South Asian Canadians (it is perhaps too much of a pipe dream to say all Canadians) across the country will be able to share the experience provided by our playwrights.

In an earlier article, "Ganga in the Assiniboine" (in *Canadian Ethnic Studies,* 1985), I have analyzed the several phases that all immigrant groups go through at both an individual and a collective level—starting with a sense of wonder at the newness of their environment and nostalgia for the land left behind, they move to a phase of hard work oblivious to all issues, and then once they are settled, they become involved with the society in which they live, and start participating in the larger community. The theatre of protest blossoms only at this stage of a community's life.

There are several problems distinct to all immigrant groups that entered Canada in the earlier half of this century. A majority were of the working classes, barely literate even in their own mother tongue; they formed self-contained communities and could prosper within them without much contact with other communities even within the same province. For example, the Icelandic community north of Winnipeg, or the Mennonite belt south and south east of Winnipeg even today have older people who speak no language other than their heritage dialect. So also with the Indo-Canadians who settled on the west coast. Mainly involved with the fruit farms and the lumber industry, they have lived in British Columbia for almost a century without assimilating into the rest of the culture. In 1971, with Bill C 31 which legally established Canada as a multicultural society, this non-assimilation was given sanction.

Teesri Duniya's beginnings

Teesri Duniya (Third World) was founded in 1981 by Rahul Varma and Rana Bose. Bose went on to form the *Serai* and I have dealt at length with Bose and *Serai* in an article that appeared in *Toronto South Asian Review* (Summer, 1988) and reprinted in *SACLIT: An Introduction* (Madras: Affiliated East West Press, 1996). Till 1985, the company produced plays in Hindi—*Julus, Ek tha*

Gadha, Bhanumati ka Pitara, Ghar Ghar ki Kahani, Ahsaas and *Darwaaze Khol Do.* In 1985, they staged *The Great Celestial Cow* in English, and a year later *On the Double,* a hilarious satire on Canadian life based on an Indian production and written by Rana Bose. It was about this time that Serai was formed.

Job Stealer was produced in 1987, *Isolated Incident* in December 1988, *Equal Wages* in 1989, *Land Where the Trees Talk* in 1990, *No Man's Land* in 1992, *Trading Injuries*, a radio-script of *No Man's Land* in 1993, and *Counter Offence* in 1996. Common to all six is *Teesri Duniya*'s standard modus operandi—to pounce on a topical controversy, and work out a script and stage a production in record time, thus capitalizing on timing and news value. The script is first written by Rahul Varma, and then workshopped and revised on a co-operative basis with other members of the company. The final scripts often bear the names of Rahul Varma and one or two others. Even when the company consisted mostly of Indo-Canadians, the dramatis personae were of various ethnocentric backgrounds, thus sending a clear message that they consider themselves spokespersons for the third world within Canadian society, namely the visible minorities who are in double jeopardy by virtue of their newness and colour. Today, *Teesri Duniya* (as also *Serai*,) has almost as many non-Indo-Canadians in their core membership as Indo-Canadians. Varma endorses the principle of colour-blind casting; that is, the actors do not have to be of the same colour or race of the characters they are portraying. In short, Othello can be played by a white actor. But can it be played without colouring his body black? Yes. A protest theatre company has to protest this imposition in order to be consistent with its mandate, and though Varma got a black actor to play a black role in *Isolated Incident*, he places more importance on the availability and skills of actors than on surface verisimilitudes. As with most protest theatre, the aim is to protest and educate, and the louder and clearer the message the closer a play comes to achieving its goals. Thus, every aspect is simplified, starting with titles that summarize the theme, and an absence of complexity in plot and characterization.

Job Stealer (1987) and *Equal Wages* (1989)

Job Stealer, like the three plays that followed it, is a full length drama that is not divided into acts or scenes. Lighting is the only way change of sets are negotiated. Also, the unities of time, place and action charted out in Aristotelian theories of drama are followed closely for purely practical reasons of pace and effect. The theme of *Job Stealer* centres around the controversy over jobs allegedly taken by refugees and immigrants from born-in-Canada Canadians.

The issue became a hot media item when a boatload of Tamils from Sri Lanka swam ashore from a German ship and asked for refugee status. The Canadian law is that all refugees are to be given asylum and monetary help, and cannot be deported without due process, that often might take months. In times of recession, the ever-simmering resentment against new immigrants and refugees erupts into angry claims that they are depriving those born in Canada of jobs or living off taxpayers' money. Add to that the charge that many are illegal aliens, and the battle becomes one against all visible minorities, regardless of their legal status. A rational look will show that immigrants, especially visible minorities or racialized minorities as is their new nomenclature, work hard and seldom ask for welfare doles. As for the Tamil boat people, the same situation might call for ballads to be written were they white and in an earlier age.

Job Stealer (the play is included in my *SACLIT Drama*) reflects the vicissitudes of all immigrants who come without a prior job offer. They suffer hardship and humiliation in the vicious circle of "No immigration without a job and no job without Canadian experience" and the sin of being overqualified. Desperate to earn something, anything, they fall prey to exploitative employers who pay them less than legal for jobs that no Canadian would care to take up anyway. Kabul, a doctor in the play who is on a sweatshop assembly line sums it up with "Besides, if it were possible to steal a job, I would have stolen a better one." The play is fast moving and picks up on all possible aspects of the situation: army brutality in the country of origin, the callousness of medical officers assigned to check up the refugees' records, of media reporters whose coverage triggers national resentment against these queue jumpers "whose reward for short-circuiting the system is instant asylum, a work permit and social benefits," of employers who send them around in circles, and of ordinary Canadians who resent them and hold them in contempt.

There is a scene in this play that is particularly noteworthy because it preceded by several months a scene by a more famous writer, Salman Rushdie. In *The Satanic Verses,* Rushdie describes the brutality of policemen hunting down alleged or suspected illegal aliens along the coast of England. In Rahul Varma's play, the government officers in the country of origin and in Canada are ruthless barbarians who assume that all non-white refugees must be carriers of syphilis or other sexually transmitted diseases. Their diction, gestures and actions are marshalled out with over-simplified exaggeration but on stage these ploys work very effectively. In all his plays, Varma inserts snatches from popular songs or tunes; in this play it is a line from Sting of the band that was much in vogue at the time—The Police. The immigration officer says, "Every move you make, every breath you take. Remember, until your status is decided I'll be watching you."

All of Varma's plays end on a note of hope and conciliation. *Job Stealer* ends with the refugees "thanking those who accepted us. The agencies and the people, and the nations . . . we came with one mouth to feed but two hands to work with." That indeed is the final truth about Canada, I agree. If you come with two hands to work with, you will survive; something that cannot be said of some other countries.

Equal Wages is dedicated to "the struggling women of the world who have broken the silence of ages." While the situation in the play could apply to many immigrant communities, especially from Asia, Varma understandably makes the key characters in his plays Indo-Canadian. The play deals with the exploitation in the garment industry; immigrant women are loaned sewing machines so they can work at home. For the women this might be a godsend in that they can stay home with their small children and yet make some money; but the other side of the equation is that employers do not incur any overheads related to maintaining a building and machinery etc. and do not have to pay any of the benefits that labour laws require. In the scene at the factory, we see exploitation of both men and women but women are much worse off in that Sly (Varma's choice of names for his characters is very obvious) harasses them with his chauvinism and sexual demands.

Isolated Incident (1988)

Isolated Incident (included in my *SACLIT Drama* anthology) is one of the most powerful of Varma's plays, both in theme and structure. It deals with the legal practice that each case should be treated as an isolated incident and is not to be tied in with any other prior act of the accused. Thus, a policeman can brutally manhandle a citizen twenty times and be acquitted each time with a mere reprimand because action cannot be taken on the pattern of brutality but only on the single incident.

The play was written for the first anniversary of the 1987 police slaying of an unarmed black youth, Anthony Griffin, in Montreal. The Griffin slaying prompted a huge public outcry and the Black Theatre Workshop prepared a script but stopped production for fear of a lawsuit. *Teesri Duniya* did not stop; it went on to get its play ready in time for the first anniversary. As with all protest theatre, the playwright draws from facts and figures to mount his case. In this play, Dexter Gibson, a young black accountant (the choice of a white collar job for him is significant for its rebuttal of stereotyping blacks) on his way to work is assaulted by white punkheads; instead of chasing them, the racist policeman, aptly named Savage, charges him and when he resists, fatally shoots him. The all-white jury acquits the police officer. Griffin was not the first victim of such injustice. In the play, Jamura lists several other recent cases, showing the pattern of police brutality. He says, "I saw Buddy Evans shot in 1978. . . . I saw Albert Johnson shot in 1979. . . . I saw J.J. Harper and Michael Wade Lawson shot in 1988, I saw Dexter . . . and now Dexter is dead." As mentioned earlier, Varma's conclusions are conciliatory. In the last scene, Dexter's mother says, "All I wish is that something good would come out of his death. . . . I want to see justice done, so that everybody, even that officer, realizes what happened was wrong." As an historical footnote, I would add that something good did come out of J.J. Harper's death. The death of this aboriginal leader in Winnipeg at the hands of a policeman gave rise to a national inquiry on the aboriginal justice system and it is hoped that the system will be revamped so that police attitudes and actions towards aboriginals, blacks and other minorities will change from arrogance and contempt to justice and cross cultural understanding.

Isolated Incident is powerful not only for its handling of police brutality but for its effective albeit raw stage directions such as the judge stepping over Dexter's body as he walks out of court. It is a well crafted play that uses such concepts from traditional Indian theatre as the storyteller, stage assistant, chorus and street magician's act. Ustad, the director or storyteller, is a woman and the play starts on a note of slapstick comedy. Jamura says he is waiting for Ustad so they can start the play. She enters, "I made it. The customs, the immigration, the security, and above all the traffic jam. But here I am, just in time." The slapstick continues as Jamura visits Balwinder Singh who is also visited by his landlord, Roach, who wants to evict him. Roach assumes Jamura is an illegal alien and calls the police who promptly leave everything else to arrest Jamura. Assuming he would be hiding, they pull the place upside down etc. etc. The playwrights mainly satirize the police and the mafia-type brotherhood that protects them from within, but they also poke fun at the various faux pas that Indian immigrants make in their ignorant efforts to conform to the society around them. All in all, *Isolated Incident* is one of his best plays. However, *Land Where the Trees Talk* is the most ambitious.

Land Where the Trees Talk (1990)

Land Where the Trees Talk was produced in September 1990, inspired by the Oka Crisis that was taking place at the time. The Oka standoff is a landmark in Canadian history though the triggering incident (a golf course that wished to expand into Indian land) seems too trivial to be true. The natives rightfully resisted the appropriation, and the matter should have been resolved with the golf course developers backing off. Who can forget the summer of 1990,—the plucky (or pesky, depending on which side one is) Mohawk warriors strategically barricading one of the arteries of traffic, being driven back and then holding out for weeks? Here is indeed material for a ballad, a saga.

Teesri Duniya had the courage to take the hot and contentious topic of Native land-rights head-on and deal with it. Varma says the 1984 Union Carbide disaster in Bhopal was his inspiration for the play. The parallels are there, he says, "it's a matter of environmental degradation linked with absence of social justice." The play is about the James Bay II project in which huge chunks of Indian land, an area bigger than France be it noted, had been appropriated by Hydro-Quebec for hydro developments which destroyed the eco-system by felling forests and polluting rivers with mercury.

The play has any number of literary and dramatic flaws. The retelling of Canadian history is a burlesque more than anything else; the whites are grossly caricatured; and his portrayal of the prime minister in the play, Chin Muldoon, comes close to courting a libel suit from Brian Mulroney of the big chin. But it is nevertheless a remarkable achievement. It tries out a variety of new stage ploys. Mother Earth is personified and the central tree is played by an Indian classical dancer. The Chief brings on stage the body of her grandson, killed by disease brought by the white man. The Chief is a woman, again reflecting contemporary trends in politics, while also being true to the role of women in Native culture. There is depiction of violence and of mercury poisoning deaths. Amid the ravages of the white man, the Indian Chief and a doctor, who is female and has a Hindu name, Karuna (Compassion), walk with compassion and dignity.

No Man's Land (1992) and its radio version, ***Trading Injuries*** (1993)

No Man's Land is about Quebec separatism, but in its radio version, it highlights the abusiveness of the workplace for immigrants trapped in sweatshops.

Himani Bannerji, in her powerful essay on the University as a site of feminist struggle, says that it took her twenty years in Canada to reach the point in her professional career that she was at when she left India, namely the point of being admitted to a tenure-track position. For those less educated, even twenty years is often not enough to get a foothold into a profession commensurate with one's training or ambition, and they get pulled down into the quicksands of mortgage payments. Varma's *Trading Injuries* combines this with the separatism politics of Quebec that is yet another dangerous roller-coaster for immigrants.

Qaizer Qureishi comes as a political refugee to Canada from strife torn Pakistan in 1970 with his wife Jeena and baby Samreen. In 1979, the rumbles of Referendum drive down real estate prices and Qaizer can afford to buy a house, or so he thinks. For the next ten years, he and Jeena work at low paying jobs in a factory in order to keep up with mortgage payments. In 1990, with another wave of separatist extremism, he is left without a job and Jeena is left with disabilities caused by workplace conditions.

The play is in twenty two scenes, and structured for audio presentation. Music has to manipulate change of scenes, especially the various flashbacks from 1970 to the present, as Jeena relives the echoes of riots in Pakistan in the upheavals of the referendum and later political unrest. The brick from the old country that Qaizer has treasured all these years becomes a symbol of the home they had hoped to have and never did, despite having a house.

Trading Injuries does not work as effectively, for me anyway, as Varma's other plays. The central situation is not as topical, the action not as hard hitting, the characters not as vibrant, as in the earlier plays.

Rahul Varma's most recent play is perhaps his best. *Counter Offence* was staged in March 1996 at the Strathearn Theatre in Montreal. It deals with yet another touchy topic—domestic violence—that becomes touchier because of the ethnic backgrounds of the main characters, a complexity that is absent in earlier plays. In *Isolated Incident,* for example, the policemen are all white and mostly racist, and the victims are all non-white. This neat white-black relationship with its inversion of the usual white (good)-black (sinful) images has very few patches of gray (one of the policeman is half-decent—I hate all equally, he says) but in *Counter Offence,* the stereotyping borders on problems. Also, Varma almost seems to argue in favour of the police by showing how Moolchand uses a charge of police racism to get a wife beater off the hook. Further, the theatre-craft used is much more complex, with the action taking place in the present, with numerous relevant flashbacks, all executed with dexterous moves of basic props comprising door frames and spotlights.

The topical issue underlying the play is the recent changes in family law and police intervention in cases of domestic violence. Many provinces now have a "zero tolerance" policy for spousal-violence. In Manitoba, for instance, the rule is that once a complaint is made, the police must pursue the case even if the victim withdraws charges. Within the play, the old rule holds: the oppressor goes scot-free if the victim refuses to press charges.

The story line is all too familiar in the social context. A man beats up his wife. A counsellor at a women's shelter helps her get the courage to break off from the relationship. A policeman, Galliard, of the family unit of the force, warns the husband, while his superior Prougault, warns Galliard not to get involved. The woman's father is concerned about family izzat, and the woman herself is torn between love for her husband that makes her withdraw charges, and her self-protective desire to be rid of him. A universal and common enough situation that one sees every time one opens a newspaper. But this play is far more complex in the specifics. The woman, Shazia, has grown up in Canada, while her parents are Muslim and from India. The husband is a student from Iran. Since he is sponsored by his wife, he can be deported if she withdraws her sponsorship. As the counsellor says, this would be a satisfying reversal of what happens to many women from outside Canada who marry abusive Canadian citizens who hold the threat of deportation over them to prevent them from lodging a complaint with the police. The counsellor is a black woman, who feels strongly about the whole issue of wife-beating.

Varma's handling of the police is the same as in *Isolated Incident*: the police chief has political ambitions; the police force works along a mafia-type "brotherhood"; the police are racist by and large; there is one good cop, Galliard. Galliard is good because he has learnt from his own childhood experience of having an abusive father who was a wife-batterer. This, incidentally, is contrary to patterns supposedly proven that the sons of abusive fathers usually become themselves abusive husbands.

However, the play is made complex by the racialization of characters. Shapoor, the wife beater is Iranian; he is a chauvinist son of a chauvinist father who controls him from half way around the world; together they want to establish a carpet trade. Shazia's father is a chauvinist and Muslim. All these—chauvinism, father-control, religion, carpet-trade—are separate entities but they tend to spill into stereotypes in audience perception. Several audience members took strong exception to Varma making his wife-beater a Muslim, and having him emotionally tied to his father's coat-tails. The most controversial character is Moolchand Misra, a community leader who befriends Shapoor for his own ends, or is it in the cause of community service? His rhetoric is powerful, and he emerges as a complex and ambiguous character. We could see him as an opportunist who uses Shapoor for his own political ends as surely as Prougault twists circumstances to his own advantage. He turns this crime against a woman to be a crime against a race, and by unfairly charging Galliard of racism helps a wife beater escape the law. On the other hand, he wants more non-whites in the police force and judiciary, and that is not an ignoble end. But one can also see the problems we face in Canada in the debate over cultural territorial rights. Galliard might antagonize some when he says, "When an ethnic smacks his wife, [must] we find a cop of matching colour and race?" But it is a very practical problem. On one hand, ethnocentric community leaders argue that cultural traits and values have to be recognized and that the larger society must keep their hands off; on the other hand, this leads to further perpetuating stereotypes such as that physical punishment in parenting is a cultural thing, or that it is culturally accepted for men to beat their wives, or that preference for male children is a cultural trait and therefore a doctor who targets South Asians for amniocenteses and subsequent abortion is blameless.

Counter Offence is a disturbing play for several reasons, not the least of which is the characterization of Moolchand as both a snake and an insightful orator.

Having built up a solid repertoire of scripts and a loyal collective of actors, and having attracted reputed directors (such as Jack Langedijke and Sally Han), *Teesri Duniya* and Rahul Varma have made a mark on the theatre scene in Montreal and South Asian Canadian literature. Next, we need a forum that would stage the plays of our playwrights across the country.

References

Uma Parameswaran, "Ganga in the Assiniboine" in *Canadian Ethnic Studies* (Summer 1985).

SACLIT Drama: Plays by South Asian Canadians. Bangalore: IBH Prakashana, 1996.

SACLIT: An Introduction to South Asian Canadian Literature. Madras: Affiliated East West Press, 1996.

This is a revised version of the essay that appeared in TSAR (Fall, 1994)

EQUAL WAGES

Helen Vlachos and Rahul Varma

Characters

1. Shyamala	An Immigrant Woman Worker
2. Pamella	A Woman Worker
3. Romila	A Woman Worker
4. Mohan Patel	Immigrant Male Worker
5. Donny	Foreman
6. Hack Saw Sly	Owner
7. Susan	Secretary
8. Mr. Shaby	Cloth Merchant
9. Rita	Shyamala's Daughter

Politician # 1, 2, 3, other Actresses/ Actors

The stage is divided into three zones. Stage right downstage is office of Sly Textile Corporation. Stage left is an area which is used for strike activity, co-op and workers meeting etc. There is a pole on stage left where posters can be hung. Preset: Few sewing machines, working table, a puncher/stapler, which is located on upstage left. Centre is where most activity takes place. Other props and settings are brought in and out of stage as required.

A woman covered in a thin veil stands with her back to the audience. A man and woman enter, in a very jovial mood. They scan the audience.

ACTOR: Do you think we have enough people to start the play?

ACTRESS: Calling it "Equal Wages" can help.

ACTOR: Maybe we could change the title—how about "Sexual Wages"? That will draw people in.

ACTRESS: Not everyone's mind is a gutter.

ACTOR: (*Giving a scornful look*) Do you realize . . . just half an hour back there wasn't anybody here. And if you think about it, many millions years ago there was nobody anywhere. So an idea struck God. After all he is sharp when it comes to ideas. And so God decided to create the moon, the sun, the stars and the planet earth . . . and on this planet earth he created forests, rivers, mountains, and all creatures including big ones like me and small ones like you.

ACTRESS: Gee, what an imagination . . . you're the best thinker I've come across in a long time.

ACTOR: God made me like that. He gave superior brains to the superior sex.

ACTRESS: Where do you get that piece of information?

ACTOR: From our sacred religious scriptures.

ACTRESS: Oh I see, that's why all the mullahs, gurus, priests and the evangelists are men. From the Ayatolla to Jimmy Swaggart.

ACTOR: Watch out miss! There are laws against women like you . . . new ones every day.

ACTRESS: And you watch out too Mr. We won't obey laws which we have no say in writing.

ACTOR: Do you think I'm making it up?

ACTRESS: Actually I do. According to a Persian poet. . . In the beginning God took a rose, a lily, a dove, a serpent, a little honey, a lion, a dead sea apple and a handful of clay. To it he added, knowledge and wisdom and when he look at his mixture, he saw a woman.

The woman in the veil turns around to pleasant music. The actress removes the veil from her and we see a Goddess image with a book, flower and a sword in her hands. The actor & actress move downstage.

ACTOR: That's what you call a woman?

ACTRESS: You don't?

ACTOR: I'll tell you what really happened. In the beginning, man roamed in jungles infested with poisonous snakes and hungry lions. He hunted food with stone weapons. He climbed mountains in the quest for fire, so that his woman can stay in the cave and cook the kill. Yes, things have changed since then, but man still holds the weapon in his hand (*Raises fist*) And deep inside his heart he still is hunter and wants his woman to stay in the cave.

ACTRESS: That's what you call a man.

ACTOR: (*Swelling with pride*)Yeah . . . What do you think?

ACTRESS: I think you can't see past the tip of your nose. Beside your fly is open. (*Actor jumps, bends, covers.*) I made you look.

They exit. Several actors creepishly walk on to the stage. In uncaring and insulting manner they take away one by one the flower, the book and the sword from the woman and replace them with broom, mop, teapot. So the woman who looked like a Goddess a moment ago looks like an everyday housewife now.

ACTOR 1: All that remains of her, now is purely womanly—washing, cleaning, cooking and breeding.

ACTOR 2: God created woman and the boredom did stop. But so did many other things. Woman was God's second mistake.

ACTOR 3: If you give God a broken heart, he will mend it. If you give woman a whole heart she will break it. If all the harm that woman has done were put in a bundle, the earth would not be able to hold it, the sky would not be able to enfold it.

ACTOR 4: Thus you may scorn them and beat them, you may live with them but cannot live without them.

ACTOR 5: I love the company of women because they are beautiful, delicate, tender and giving. But what I like most in a woman is her silence.

Hush which slowly turns into loud music. The veiled woman throws the broom and mop etc. The actors freeze in an abstract formation.

WOMAN: I AM NO
Weakling cowed by society.
No traditional kitten in the kitchen,
No tender shoot shot down by manslaughter,
No branch broken, helpless in the master's courtyard,
No signed flower in the office and the factory.

I AM NO MORE
The helpless living there,
Suppressed by men
Crushed by bars,
In the name of culture, stuff of trade

NO MORE
The living corpse of the kitchen, bedroom and street.

I AM
The power seizing her right
One half of struggling people.
I am raising my head, shattering the silence of ages,
I AM A WOMAN.

All actors come downstage. Face the audience.

MAN: We dedicate tonight's play to the women of the world.
WOMAN: We salute the struggling women of the world who have broken the silence of ages. And so we present our play called "Equal Wages."

All exit. An immigrant woman, Shyamala, in her late middle age enters; she packs up pieces in boxes, tapes them and writes numbers on them and piles them one over the other. Suddenly she leaves the boxes, goes to kitchen, puts on water and packs a lunch bag. Returns to boxes again. Packs one and goes back to switch off stove. Daughter [Rita] about 20 who is perturbed with all this noise early in the morning arrives from her sleep.

RITA: Hello mother.
SHYAMALA: You are up? Already?
RITA: In this house one does not need an alarm clock to get up—your clanking the pots and stacking up the boxes does the job.
SHYAMALA: Sorry honey, I have to finish before the boss comes to pick them up or else he'll hire someone else.
RITA: Let him. At least you can rest a bit.
SHYAMALA: Rest? Who will pay off this house?

RITA: Mother you are always working to pay off this house—You hardly have any time for anything else, you don't even have time for me.

SHYAMALA: That's all I need to hear.

RITA: When did you have time to sit with me? When did you have time to see my teacher? You know what Mr. Thompson says, your parents are too busy piling up dollars, they haven't got time for you.

SHYAMALA: If he only knew, that the factory is not just my job, it's my prison.

There is a knock at the door.

That must be Mr. Shaby come to collect boxes . . . Oh God . . .

She rushes to open doors. The Boss Mr. Shaby with his characteristic mean smile steps in.

Good morning Mr. Shaby.

SHABY: Finished Shyamala?

SHYAMALA: Would you care for a cup of tea Mr. Shaby?

SHABY: (*Nodding his head in yes*) . . . Thank you . . . All done? (*He walks close to boxes*)

SHYAMALA: (*Shyamala stacks up one more box*) Almost.

SHABY: Almost?

SHYAMALA: I had to work a long shift yesterday and as you know I am in no position to refuse.

SHABY: (*With hurting sarcasm*) Don't I know that . . . overtime pays time and half.

SHYAMALA: No it's not that. It is if I don't go when they call me . . . I can't go at all.

SHABY: (*Sipping tea, sadistically*) . . . you know another boatload of refugees have arrived. . . . Haitians. . . . If you can't

Shyamala cuts in

SHYAMALA: No. . . . I will do your work.

SHABY: And their women work for less.

SHYAMALA: But I've been working hard for you

Shaby looks at unfinished work.

Mostly I'm on time and I do good work.

SHABY: Oh sure . . . but the new arrivals have to be looked after.
SHYAMALA: (*mumbles*)
SHABY: You aren't against them getting jobs. . . . Are you? (*Shyamala's silence*) All my life I've given employment to new arrivals and I have paid them on time and they have worked on time. Don't you think that's fair.
SHYAMALA: Yes Mr. Shaby!
SHABY: And it's only fair that I pay you the same as I pay them; Equal pay for Equal work . . . don't you agree.
SHYAMALA: I'll be finished these new ones first thing in the morning.
SHABY: That's a good girl. Let me load these in my station wagon.

Shyamala helps him. He dumps a big bag full of pieces.

Mainly style B, size 7 to 11. (*He is leaving*)
SHYAMALA: Mr. Sly (*He stops*) I don't want to be rude but do you think you could pay me today.
SHABY: (*With a smile*) When the job's done you'll get your money. . . . (*stepping out*) By the way thanks for the tea.

He exits. Rita enters.

RITA: Son of a bitch.
SHYAMALA: Rita you are learning western ways.
RITA: Why do you have to work in the factory as well as at home for this creep.
SHYAMALA: Because working twice as hard, I can make as much money as a man.
RITA: Money, money, money. . . . Is there anything else in life?
SHYAMALA: Yes taxes . . . (*a horn is heard*) That must be Pamella . . . come to pick me up.

RITA: Is she still going out with what's his name . . . Donny.

SHYAMALA: Yes. They're still not married but act as though they are. Otherwise she is a good girl. (*Horn again*) I have to run. Can you pack those pieces.

Shyamala quickly kisses her and exits. Rita fixes things behind her and leaves.

People begin to mass outside the factory some drinking coffee from thermos and some carrying their lunch bags. Donny who is standing ahead of everyone begins to cross his legs and bends.

MOHAN: What's wrong?

DONNY: I've got to take a leak.

MOHAN: Why don't you go?

DONNY: And lose my place to you for a lousy leak.

MOHAN: Don't hold your leak pal. I'll keep your place for you. . . . Trust me I will.

Donny thanks him, moves to upstage, relieves himself and returns feeling good.

DONNY: So what is that you do?

MOHAN:Unemployed.

DONNY: Unemployed at what?

MOHAN: Anything you name it. I apply to all job openings from the career pages of the newspaper . . . some would call for an interview.

Shyamala cuts into the conversation.

SHYAMALA: And in the interview they would ask "Do you have Canadian experience." And if you say . . .

Motions him to answer.

MOHAN: No.

SHYAMALA: They'll say no Canadian experience, no job.

MOHAN: That's right, but how did you know?

SHYAMALA: That's my Canadian experience.

Pamella enters and joins the line. Donny runs to her.

DONNY: How's my Juliette today.
PAMELLA: Couldn't sleep last night.
DONNY: Did you dream about me?
PAMELLA: To dream I had to sleep.
DONNY: Tell me you love me.
PAMELLA: Are you stupid or are you just acting like it.
DONNY: Last night you said you loved me.
PAMELLA: It I did, it was shortlived.
DONNY: How about a hamburger tonight and then maybe . . . com'on it'll be a blast.

Sly coming in.

PAMELLA: He is coming.
DONNY: Who is coming?
PAMELLA: The boss.
DONNY: The bloodsucker. He promised me a raise last year, I'm still waiting.
SLY: Morning men, Morning ladies and welcome to Sly Textile Corporation. . . . I'm Hacksaw Sly, did you know my name? I know you did. My business is Fabrics it's difficult business-those with guts dare stick around. You people got guts?

All nod their heads in approval.

I know you do. I want people who believe in hard work and not in paper-work. I want people who love their work . . . will you love your work? . . .

All nod their heads in approval.

So will you accept the company wages?

All confused/ questioning.

I know you would.

The workers hesitantly nod their head in approval.

So will you Hurry up . . . Waste not time. . . . Time is money. . . . Hurry up.

Sly is picking workers to hire.

SLY: Hey you, what's your name?

Mohan steps forward.

MOHAN: Mohan Patel.
SLY: Father is also Patel.
MOHAN: Sohan Patel.
SLY: Age?
MOHAN: 30.
SLY: Sex?
MOHAN: 4 times a week.
SLY: (*Aside*) And in Quebec they complain about declining birth rates? (*To Mohan*) Welcome to Sly Textile Corporation. Next!

Romila steps forward.

Name?
ROMILA: Romila.
SLY: Age?
ROMILA: 32.
SLY: Sex?

Romila looks at her, Sly scans his eyes on her body.

Okay. Okay . . . married?
ROMILA: What is that got to do with the job?
SLY: I don't want to see a mother on the job, while junior cries for milk.

Romila sensing the loss.

ROMILA: Married. . . . I don't know. . . . I mean unmarried . . . yeah unmarried.

SLY: Welcome to Sly Textile Corporation. . . . Hurry up. . . . Next.

Sly hires few of them. He mimes starting a power line and all the workers form a human machine, miming work. They sing as they work.

ONE: Sly.
ALL: Sly.
ONE: Textile.
ALL: Textile.
ONE: Corporation.
ALL: Corporation.
ONE: Sly Textile Corporation.
ALL: Sly Textile Corporation.
ONE: Cheap wages and exploitation.
ALL: Cheap wages and exploitation.

They repeat "corporation—exploitation" . . . faster and faster until Sly mimes power shut down. All stop.

SLY: Coffee break . . . thanks of The Govt. of Canada. You can take a leak, or feast on that food you always bring. . . . What was it again—dandelions?

Mohan and Donny go for leak. Donny returns to Pamella. Mohan returns and lies flat on the ground. Romila sits down to eat. Shyamala cuts coupons from newspaper.

SHYAMALA: (*To Romila*) Romila, I thought you hated pickles.
ROMILA: But I like them now.
SHYAMALA: Is it my imagination or are you putting on weight. (*Romila feels her stomach*) Your face looks bigger.
ROMILA: It's nothing . . . women have days like this.
SHYAMALA: (*Probing*) Are you . . .

Romila gets up and leaves saying "excuse." Pamella fixes hair. Donny returns to Pamella.

PAMELLA: (*To Shyamala*) I think she is . . .
DONNY: (*To Pamella*) You look pretty even when you are tired.
PAMELLA: Cool it Romeo. I've got work to do.
DONNY: Marry me and you won't have to.
PAMELLA: But I like to work.
DONNY: Now that's a good reason to get married.
PAMELLA: No thank you. . . . I can't see myself slaving here and cooking and cleaning at home.
DONNY: At least it would be for your own husband and your own house.
PAMELLA: Why don't you wipe that fog off your glasses.

She takes off his glasses and leaves.

DONNY: What is it? Is it another man . . . Shit.

Donny goes and lies near Mohan. Sly walks over to Shyamala.

SLY: Shyamala.
SHYAMALA: Yes, Mr. Sly.
SLY: Call me Hacks.
SHYAMALA: Mr. Hacks Sly.
SLY: Just Hacks.
SHYAMALA: Yes, Mr. Just Hacks.
SLY: (*Flabbergasted*). . . How you doing Shyamala?
SHYAMALA: Couldn't be better—bleeding nose, swollen feet, aching back. . . . Can't complain, how are you?
SLY: My financial situation stinks.
SHYAMALA: Mine is worst.
SLY: Then don't eat meat.
SHYAMALA: Are you kidding? I can't even remember what it looks like. Can't even afford to buy a box of chicken base without a discount coupon (*shows him discount coupons*) I'm bled to death with these high prices. Mr. Sly do you think you could give us a raise.

Pamella who has just returned.

PAMELLA: Yes Sly . . . we just had a raise in rents.
SLY: So did I.
PAMELLA: You own a bungalow.
SLY: I had a raise in cheap imports from Hong Kong. Those petite chinks drive my profits down. Beside my expenses and supplies are too high, plus I have other responsibilities like my dues to the Golf Club. Try to put yourself in my shoes and you'll know what I mean.
PAMELLA: You're on. I will trade places with you. You come down and I'll go up.
SLY: Do you know what goes up and never comes down.
ROMILA: (*From distance*) My weight.
SLY: (*Snubbing*) Inflation. It hit a 5 year high and all because . . .
DONNY: Mismanagement.
MOHAN: Govt. Incompetence.
SHYAMALA: Double whamming of federal tax.
PAMELLA: Hefty provincial tax.
ROMILA: Free trade.
SLY: You are all blabbering idiots. It's becuase of your high wages.
SHYAMALA: You call $4.65 an hour high wages?
SLY: Well it's 10 cents higher since the last raise. Plus you guys always expect wage parity, and indexing.
SHYAMALA: And why not? That MPs have their salaries adjusted to inflation each year.
ROMILA: Mr. Sly, last time I remember our wages going up was before general election.
SLY: Enough! I can't give you a raise. This year my profits are way down.
SHYAMALA: Next thing you'll tell us is . . .
SLY: Your wages are frozen.
SHYAMALA: That's what I feared.
ROMILA: I would like to see prices frozen for a change.
SHYAMALA: Mr. Sly! there must be other ways to make profits other than freezing our already low wages.
SLY: That's the next thing I was going to tell you . . . (*All eager to hear*) Lay-off.

Shocked.

SLY: Shyamala.
SHYAMALA: Yes Mr. Sly.
SLY: You are no longer needed.
SHYAMALA: Excuse me?
SLY: You are fired.
SHYAMALA: (*Stunned*) You can't be serious.
SLY: Oh I am.
SHYAMALA: Mr. Sly I work hard.
SLY: Good.
SHYAMALA: I give money to the company's X-mas fund even though I don't celebrate.
SLY: I am impressed.
SHYAMALA: I get along fine with all white women even though I'm paid less than them.
SLY: Are you accusing me of paying you less than I do white women. My dear Shyamala . . . in Sly Textile Corporation black, brown, yellow, every woman's a nigger.
SHYAMALA: And I never complain.
SLY: What do you think you're doing. I'll have to let you go. (*To Pamella*) . . . Pamella she was complaining against you. . . . I fired her.
PAMELLA: Mr. Sly, you've got to give her at least 7 days notice.
SLY: (*Upset*) I've got to but I won't. If she wants, she can go to labour complaint board. But she would be better off going to the unemployment board. And my dear Pamella . . . you'd be better off holding on to your job as long as you have it . . . because you never know what can happen next.

All silent. Workers heading to their places. Sly mimes power on.

30 seconds and back to work.
DONNY: Sly is good man except he is guided by profits.
ROMILA: I feel sorry for Shyamala. She was a good worker.
SLY: Hurry up . . .

The workers resume their work. Shyamala walks across the stage with a sign which reads "Hired Last Fired First." She hangs the sign on the pole. Workers sing as they work.

SONG: If you want a job to make some money.
Get-off your ass and work with us honey
Wages are low and the profits are high.
Work as a slave until you die.
No job protection—prices going up.
We got pissed-off, we got fed up.
So we went up to the boss and told that clown
Raise our wages or face slow down.

They all stop.

SLY: What is that?
ALL:Slow down.
SLY:I call it sagging profits. You damn well know that you're just transients but you behave like unionized creeps. Listen, so far I've been very nice to pay you when I'm supposed to and there is even toilet paper in the toilets. But I can't toleratre a slow down. Because that cuts into my profits and I get depressed. If I don't make profits, I will have to move the company to a more profitable place, like Taiwan. So you either wise up or face a shut down. . . . And don't test my patience.

He points at Shyamala, the workers forced to resume work. Romila and Pamella on the machine. Donny is doing the Invoice. Mohan carrying boxes on trolley and stacking up. He notices trolley broken. Tries to fix.

Hey Mohan Patel.
MOHAN: Mohan Patel Sir.
SLY: You bilingual?
MOHAN: At least Sir, and I speak French too.
SLY: What's the problem?
MOHAN: The wheel is wobbly. I need a new trolley.

SLY: What do you think? The company is some kind of money tree, that I'll go on buying and you'll go on breaking. Nobody else breaks except you.

MOHAN: Right sir, because nobody else clears the warehouse and unloads the trucks.

Mohan pushes the wobbly trolley. He drags his feet.

SLY: Why are you dragging your leg?

MOHAN: My knee is bothering me today.

SLY: How long have you been doing this work—10 years?

MOHAN: Five and I am already half crippled.

SLY:You'll get used to it.

MOHAN: What? being cripple?

SLY: No, the work.

MOHAN: It's bad enough that I get jobs nobody else wants. . . . And then I'll be blamed. . . .

SLY: Wait a minute. What's the exchange rate between dollar and the currency of the country you came from?

MOHAN: One dollar is 12 rupees.

SLY:Which means you earn 12 times more which means here is one month you'll earn the same as you'll earn in one year in India. So why are you complaining?

MOHAN: But I pay taxes here. Do you mind if I live by the rules of this country?

SLY: (*Aside*) A worker with a touch of politics. (*To Mohan*) Okay. Go load those boxes in this country.

MOHAN: But my leg. . . .

SLY: I'm telling you—load it boy. If you don't like it leave it.

MOHAN: Which means either I ruin my knees, or I starve.

SLY: Which means before you hit me for a work related accident, I'll relieve you.

MOHAN: I don't understand.

SLY: Mohan.

MOHAN: Sly.

SLY: You're fired.

MOHAN: (*Panicked*) Sly, I've got children, I've got to work. I'm working for food.

SLY: Blame it on the slow down. As for the rest of you better wise-up or you know where you'll end up.

Points at Mohan who is joining Shyamala with a sign which reads "Unemployed Cheap Labour."

understood. . . . Got the message.

Workers express sorry and Sly gives mean laugh. Workers sing as they work.

SONG: Our noses bleed but still we're alive.
If you can't cope, you won't survive.
Sound of one, two, three, four. One, two, three, four.
These low wages just don't fit.
Bossman he don't give a shit.

SLY: Donny.

DONNY: Yes Mr. Sly.

SLY: Bring that cart down.

DONNY: (*Shocked*) . . . you expect me to move stuff around.

SLY: Got that Donny?

Donny pushes the trolley which Mohan had left. Before Donny is finished.

Donny go downstairs to the shipping. See if supplies are in.

DONNY: Me . . . Shipping . . . Supplies?

SLY: And after that, there's packing.

DONNY: Sly—you're giving me work I never did before.

SLY: Who told you that?

DONNY: Nobody's got to tell me. I know what's my job.

SLY: Donny I hired you to do the invoices yes. But I am responsible for making decisions around here. Have I made myself clear?

DONNY: Yes.

SLY: Good. . . Get going.

Donny does invoices and leaves for shipping. Romila sorts clothing. Pamella works on machine. Sly orders around Romila.

How many skirts we got . . . size 9?
ROMILA: (*Checking*) About 100.
SLY: Size 10?
ROMILA: One rack full.
SLY: Any shorts left.
ROMILA: 20 or so. On the top shelf.
SLY: Pull them down and pack.

Romila upset. But follows. Phone rings. Sly picks up.

(*On the phone*) . . . 10 Cents? Govt. memo? Well we have to jack up the prices.

Romila in the mean time works sitting down.

Good news fellahs. The Govt. has legislated a 10 cents increase and it's not even election time. So that raises your minimum wages to 4.75 maxmium.

PAMELLA: 10 cents sure covers the cost of living?
ROMILA: For all I care, my work load is increased faster than 10 cents raise, with half the workers laid-off.
SLY: Aren't you happy you aren't one of them.
ROMILA: Happy about what? Doing work of two people alone.
SLY: Right. That's efficient management. Now make it a point to exactly know what we have in stock or is that too much to ask?
ROMILA: I'm packing.
SLY: But why are you sitting down?
ROMILA: Because I work better sitting down.
SLY: Make sure you know what's in the stock.
ROMILA: I don't have to. I'm not shipper.
SLY: What do you think you're doing? Acting in a Charlie Chaplin movie? Move that cart and stack up. What a little extra work for you. . . . Be a woman or you know where you will end up.

Points at fired workers. Romila starts pushing the trolley and stacking up. Suddenly she stops and sits down holding her waist, leaving the trolley she was pushing.

SLY: Who ask you to stop.

Romila panting.

You don't get paid to sit down.

Romila motions to wait.

Get back to stacking.

Pamella comes to Romila.

PAMELLA: She is feeling sick.
SLY: It's not time to feel sick. In Sly Textile Corporation workers feel sick only on Sundays.

Pamella checking her stomach.

Move those 10's on the self.
PAMELLA: She can't. She is feeling sick.
SLY: She is faking.
PAMELLA: She isn't faking. She is pregnant.
SLY: I don't see her stomach bulging.
PAMELLA: It's something you won't understand.
SLY: She can't be pregnant. That's not compatible with her job.
PAMELLA: You better give her this afternoon off and move her to lighter work.
SLY: Two big orders came on urgent request from New York.
PAMELLA: So let them wait.
SLY: I can't fool around with New York order with free trade and all.
PAMELLA: Why not?
SLY: Why not what?
PAMELLA: She is pregnant.
SLY: You're getting 10 cents increase.
PAMELLA: Big deal. It goes off in taxes.
SLY: I don't care. . . . New York orders me and I order you and you do it . . . and that is all. And you know what else I do. . . . I hire and fire around here . . . remember that.

PAMELLA: She is going to have a baby.

SLY: She is going to give birth to her replacement.

ROMILA: What do you mean?

SLY: I ask the questions here, girl. If you can't do the work, leave it.

ROMILA: Excuse me?

SLY: You're fired.

PAMELLA: She is not fired, she needs maternity leave.

SLY: She needs permanent leave. . . . Next thing you are going to say, she needs day care. What do you think I'm running, business or charity?

PAMELLA: There are laws Sly.

SLY: And there are flaws Pamella.

PAMELLA: She can go to authorities you know.

SLY: (*Mimes as he talks*) Be my guest. Go to authorities. Take a number and wait 2 hours before the receptionist calls her "Mrs. Romila, Mr. Kidworth is ready to see you. Please go through. On your right there are steps with a sign 'No Admission,' walk right through. On your right there are steps with a sign saying 'Don't Cross,' jump over. Right in the hall is sign which reads 'Silence Please,' you yell there Mr. Kidworth will come out to see you." And I can tell you what he will tell her. He will tell her to go to the grievance board and the grievance board will tell her to go to the doctor and the doctor will give her a letter advising light work and she will bring the letter to me and I will tell her, there ain't light work here. Then she will go back to the grievance board, who will send her to the lawyer and she will lose every single penny of her savings paying off the lawyer and then she will think back, "was it really worth running around."

PAMELLA: Pimp!

Romila joins the unemployed. She picks up sign reading "Axed due to maternity."

SLY: Now the axe won't fall on you, if you took your day's worth and kept your mouth shut. And here is your day's worth subtracting U.I. and income tax.

PAMELLA: Income tax? We have to have income to pay income tax.

SLY: Cute! Taking away income tax, power tax, thumb tax and company tax.

PAMELLA: Company tax?

SLY: For the clocks, so you can see when coffee break is. So with usual deduction $40 for Donny and $29.99 for Pamella.

PAMELLA: $29.99?

SLY: Why do you always scream and squeak?

PAMELLA: I want equal wages.

SLY: Equal to whom?

PAMELLA: Him.

SLY: Be serious Pamella.

PAMELLA: I work as much.

SLY: You are nervous, stressed, undependable, and less productive. Besides you have hormonal imbalances.

PAMELLA: I except to get equal wages or else.

SLY: Or else What?

PAMELLA: You have a fight on your hand Mister.

SLY: Tell me about it.

PAMELLA: Look Sly. . . . I took a lot of crap from you. You've been firing us and breaking rules, and I ignored you. But when you challenge just not me but whole womankind, as if they are less than human, I challenge you to come out open and fight like a man.

SLY: Oh really? How do you plan to fight.

PAMELLA: We are gonna walk-off the job.

SLY: Strike?

PAMELLA: Yeah.

SLY: Get serious.

PAMELLA: We are doing it.

SLY: You got no rights.

PAMELLA: You got no right to tell us that.

SLY: Do you remember what happened in the last strike? You were on news watch for 14 seconds that's all.

PAMELLA: Won't be the same this time--you remember my face and mark my words. I'll come back haunting you.

SLY: Pamella you're fired.

PAMELLA: Shove it.

Pamella picks up sign which reads "Equal wages for Equal work." As she is about to leave Donny comes running to her.

DONNY: Pamella let's talk it out.

PAMELLA: Donny let's walk out.

DONNY: I mean we don't want to lose our job.

PAMELLA: We have always been losing on job. It's about time to fight it to win.

DONNY: Against Sly Textile Corporation?

PAMELLA: And anybody else who pay women less than men.

DONNY: Pamella I understand that you girls are upset, but these things do happen. The Govt and the rich and all are working on that. In the meanwhile. . . . I mean when the work is there it is there and when it's not it's not.

PAMELLA: Spare me your bullshit Romeo.

DONNY: Lots of rush orders this time of the year . . . lots of overtime.

PAMELLA: Yeah. Why do I have to do overtime—60 hours a week to make as much as you do during regular hours.

DONNY: You can't beat them. They are all big men.

PAMELLA: We just have to fight harder. Wasn't it you who said bosses are different from us when he didn't give you the raise he promised you.

DONNY: Yeah . . . becuase I deserved higher wages.

PAMELLA: And I don't deserve equal wages. Is that what you're saying me-that we aren't equal to each other and you expect me to marry you?

DONNY: Think about it. Would you want me to lose my job for something like equal wages, when we can get married and live happily ever after. What differnce does it make if the second pay cheque is a few dollars less?

PAMELLA: What you call second pay-cheque, is the only cheque many women have in the family. Get it into your head that a job done deserves the same pay and the same cheque.

DONNY: But I won't mind the second cheque, I'll still love you and you can still buy your luxuries.

PAMELLA: You're losing your brain when you need it.

DONNY: You're losing your brain . . . you're not going to get anywhere carrying that sign.

Tries to read the sign.

SLY: Don't listen to her Donny, she's jealous. What does it read?

Looks for his glasses and doesn't realize he's wearing them.

DONNY: Where are my glasses?
PAMELLA: Gone with your brain.

She pulls the glasses, flips in air and spits. Donny runs, picks up glasses and catches her arm.

It's the beginning of the end Donny.

DONNY: Beginning of what?
PAMELLA: 500 women on strike.
DONNY: And end of what?
PAMELLA: You and me.
DONNY: You would dump a man who loves you so much for 500 striking women.
SLY: *[Butting in]* And you'd forget about beautiful life you can start with him if you don't go on strike.

Pamella nods "yes."

Well it's too bad, because only a blind donkey doesn't see the darkness.
PAMELLA: *[To Donny]* Only a blind donkey doesn't see the light.

She spits and puts "Equal wages. . . " sign at most prominent spot on the pole and Donny stands helplessly.

SLY: Don't worry Donny. If she really loved you, she wouldn't have dumped you. I have the feeling that she hates tall men because she is the type who don't want to look up to one, she prefers to look down upon them but as it happens . . . men are taller. Anyway let them walk out and you stay in.

DONNY: You mean be a strike breaker.

SLY: Yes they'll call you a pimp but that won't matter because you can't be a foreman and a nice guy at the same time. And they'll picket you but that won't matter either because the police will guard you. And when the company brings in scabs that won't matter either because you'd be better as a foreman than them striking cry-baby communists.

Donny dances and sings.

DONNY: I'm feeling fine, cause all the jobs are mine.
He made me a promise, He'll make me foreman.
He's the man with the most and I'll drive his van.
I conspire I perspire like a son of a bitch.
I say it's me who is getting rich.
I got it made, cause all home gals ran
Now I'm gonna be a foreman.

SLY: Now clean-up striker's mess. The distributor and Daisy should be here soon.

DONNY: Daisy?

SLY: Model from New York. She sweats and starves to keep in shape and boy what shapely round breasts and splendid better padded part of anatomy she's got. When she models a dress, the girls go crazy even they haven't got her figure and beauty . . . but what the heck sales go up anyway.

DONNY: Really!

SLY: But Susan is as pretty.

DONNY: Susan?

SLY: My Secretary.

They exit. Susan enters arranges office and goes out to bring something.

(*Off Stage*) . . . Susan.

Sly enters with Donny.

Susan.

He sprays deodorant in his armpits.

SUSAN: (*Off stage*) Just a moment Mr. Sly.

SLY: Half the time she is in the ladies room putting on make-up, next she will fall in love, get married and cost the company money in maternity benefits. Oh these women, you can't leave anything on them. . . .

Susan enters. Heads for Sly's desk and relays info. in official manner. Sly is frozen/mesmerized with her efficiency. He keeps nodding his head like a chameleon as Susan talks.

SUSAN: Good morning Mr. Sly, I have the financial statement ready. The profits continued to rise this quarter, but as in last quarter, just barely, meaning a long expected slow down is underway. . . . GDP rose erratically and the inflation numbers show a slow movement towards recession . . . and the wage freeze. . . .

Sly motions her to stop by raising his hand. Remain frozen and after a pause. . . .

SLY: I know.

SUSAN: (*Aside*) Do you? (*To Sly*) Just refreshing your memory.

Sly gets up and moves close behind her.

SUSAN: (*Escaping*) . . . Coffee Mr. Sly?

Sly follows her to coffee machine. Stands close behind her. She escapes to desk by saying . . .

Dictation Mr. Sly?

Susan picks up writing pad and Sly again places himself against her.

SLY: No dictation today.

He takes away the pad. Blocks her way from escaping, but she manages to free herself. Walks away. Sly displeased, frustrated throws himself on chair.

SUSUAN: Well Mr. Sly . . . the financial statement was typed, updated, and compiled yesterday.
SLY: Filed?
SUSAN: I would have filed it yesterday too, but estimates had to be typed urgently . . . because the estimator Mr. Moosehead said he **had a meeting.**
SLY: So . . . you're doing fine.

He stands again and comes leaning on her.

SUSAN: And if you excuse me I've got to send fax to New York.

She escapes.

SLY: (*Retorts back*) Susan shorthand.
SUSAN: You said no shorthand today.
SLY: I changed my mind.
SUSAN: (*aside*) Does the new one work any better?

She picks up writing pad.

Okay Mr. Sly . . .?
SLY: What did I just say?
SUSAN: Nothing so far.
SLY: Let me rephrase it. It doesn't sound good.

Pretending to think. Sly keeps chasing/ leaning/ feeling her and she keeps escaping until Sly finally dictates. Susan takes notes faster than Sly can talk. It is like "who is faster game" between the two.

SLY: Addressed to . . . Buster Douglas, Chief of Police, Public order maintenance section. Provincial police force. Dear Chief Buster, in spite of serious attempts to avoid strike . . . negotiations have failed . . . probably because in the last few years we are seeing a new breed of workers—women.

Sly and Susan exchange stare.

Before, migrants walked right off the boat and walked to factory. They knew their job and respected the rules. Now they don't obey the rules of the game.

Exchange stare.

That's where you come in. To crush . . . no strike that out Susan. . . . To eject out the socially undesirable elements in other words shit disturbers . . . no strike that out too . . . in this case women who are forcing peaceful workers to walk off the job.

They exchange looks.

There is fear of safety of those who would want to work.

SUSAN: Scabs.

SLY: What?

SUSAN: Just a sneeze . . . excuse me.

SLY: I heard scab.

She motions "no."

Therefore I request proper protection be provided to willing workers. Signed. Hacksaw Sly.

Susan is not a second late in taking shorthand. And looking at him as though asking "What's next." Sly moves away while Susan heads for the typewriter.

Type . . . make several copies . . . send one to city hall.

And we hear typewriter going 1000 wpm. Susan is back.

SUSAN: . . . This one is for the police chief . . . this for the chief minister . . . this for the chamber of commerce . . . you sign bottom left-hand side.

Sly surprised.

SLY: All done?

SUSAN: Could have finished earlier but I had to reserve your flight to New York.

SLY: Okay . . . How are the boys in accounting.

SUSAN: Out to lunch.

SLY: Must be meeting customers.

SUSAN: Therefore I did the expenses. But I couldn't send the pay cheques to the workers because chief accountant Mr. Holyfield said to hold the cheques.

SLY: Did you?

SUSAN: Yes.

SLY: Good. You're better than the boys in accounting.

SUSAN: And cheap too.

Sly looks at garbage bin.

SLY: How come the garbage is overflowing.

SUSAN: (*Aside*) . . . Because tons of garbage going around the room. (*To Sly*) . . . The women in cleaning have walked off job. They want wage parity with the janitors.

SLY: This is getting out of hand. These women think that all they got to do is walk-off the job and I'll come begging them to return. But they better know and know good that a truck load of workers will be joining us tomorrow.

SUSAN: You mean scabs.

SLY: I call them willing workers who love their families. (*Pause*) Why do I get the feeling that you are a strike supporter.

SUSAN: Oh I am sorry. I didn't realize I'm so expressive, but I guess it means I support them.

SLY: Who is poisoning your mind? You dress up as you want, the make-up what you like, smile when you want. . . .

SUSAN: And I keep my legs crossed when I get flowers, and go on vacation when there is ticket sale but inside I don't like it.

SLY: Isn't that something. You should be happy doing the light work—typing and smiling.

SUSAN: So here I leave you with heavy work . . . giving orders.

SLY: What is that supposed to mean.

SUSAN: You won't harass me any further because I'm walking off and so are many other girls.

Susan going to join the striker with a sign which reads "Harassment." Row of girls walks across saying good bye to Sly.

SLY: This strike is contagious. Now who would do all the correspondence, bills, conference calls, shorthand, accounting, faxing, xeroxing, tabulation estimation and management.

DONNY: (*Aside*) And harassment. (*To Sly*) This is not fun. All the pretty broads are gone.

SLY: I have to get to the Chamber of Commerce, before it goes completely out of hand.

He exits. Donny follows the women set up banner "Strike support co-op. All mass up in front of the banner signs, placards etc. Susan brings whole bag full of supplies of canned food, coffee soup etc.

PAMELLA: You are an inspiration to the strike. Collecting donations for co-op. I wish we had more girls like you.

SUSAN: There are many. Some girls are setting up a Bazaar, some a garage sale, some are going door to door; even the executive wives club is throwing a fund raising ball.

PAMELLA: And messages of support pouring in (*She begins to pull letters*) from women union of West Coast, Women action commence in Quebec. . . . Immigrant Women's aid. Some have even sent contribution.

The women rejoice.

But don't be so happy. We've also got a notice from the city to move the co-op because . . . (*She reads notice*) . . . "illegal occupation of city property can cause chaos in normal running of civic affair" . . .can you believe that.

SHYAMALA: They can't do that. This co-op means so much to girls.

SUSAN: And that means I won't go collecting donations. I will get a court injunction today.

SHYAMALA: Somebody should put injunction on scabs.

PAMELLA: You can hardly call them scabs. Those are few out of town retired ladies who give-up after one hour.

Romila enters.

Hey Romila, did you see your doctor?

ROMILA: Yes, it's a girl.

SHYAMALA: Maybe we should name her "Strike."

ROMILA: I don't think I can go on strike much longer. I need money for the baby.

PAMELLA: I don't think you'd want to see your girl born as underpaid slave. If we can hold on we are gonna win this strike for all womankind.

ROMILLA: It's different for you—you don't have a family and husband.

SUSAN: She isn't pregnant either.

ROMILA: Do you want me to live on a bowl of soup and dollar a day strike fund.

SHYAMALA: No, we don't, certainly not. Becuase we don't get that much more. Romila it's hard on us . . . and especially hard on you. We knew it wasn't going to be a picnic.

SUSAN: Except for executive wives club.

SHYAMALA: That's why I never joined a strike before. But now seeing women from all over of all colours . . . it feels good being together . . . because we have realized all women are treated as second class citizens regardless of colour.

MOHAN: But the company can outlast strike. Can we? We are against big guys and I don't think we can beat them.

SHYAMALA: So what do you want to do? Join them?

MOHAN: We've sustained strike for months. We've got national attention. We can be proud of that. If we return back, we still have set the issue on agenda. That's not being beaten.

SHYAMALA: That's surrender.

MOHAN: If we stay out, they will move the company to South Korea. Where are we going to go . . . welfare?

PAMELLA: It's one thing for you to go back. You were making a dollar more than us.

MOHAN: So for that one dollar we all have to live on dollar a day strike fund.

PAMELLA: Mohan, if you want to go back, nobody's stopping you.

MOHAN: At least by going back we can stop the company from moving to South Korea.

All argue chaotically. Sly enters in his office with Donny. The workers subside.

SLY: What's this pounding on my ear drums.

From the strikers, side arguments "You don't understand . . . etc." are heard.

DONNY: The women are telling each other that they don't understand anything.

SLY: (*Aside*) Passion drying out. (*To Donny*) Do you understand that?

DONNY: What?

SLY: A month ago they were saying "strike, strike. Equal wage for equal work . . . justice. . . ." Now is the time to strike a deal.

DONNY: I don't understand.

SLY: I am going to rehire 100 striking women back.

DONNY: 100 of them?

SLY: On second thoughts 200, since I pay them half the wages.

DONNY: I doubt they'll accept old wages.

SLY: A poor widow will marry any old man. In the Chamber of Commerce I learned a dividing trick, strike a deal with a big stick.

DONNY: Now I am really lost.

SLY: That's why you are Donny and I'm Sly.

He whispers in Donny's ears. Donny takes a walk towards the strikers.

DONNY: Ladies, ladies, I have brought you a dandy offer—the company is willing to rehire you provided you call off the strike.

PAMELLA: What's the catch Donny?

DONNY: The company will give you 25 cents an hour increase across the table to everyone.

Surprise, whispers . . .

ROMILA: I'll take it.

MOHAN: I don't mind either . . . 25 cents . . .

SHYAMALA: I smell a rat . . . what's the catch?

DONNY: There are only 200 jobs.

SHYAMALA: And what about the other 300.

PAMELLA: And what about equal wages.

Donny gives her mean look.

DONNY: We are talking 25 cents extra equally distributed across the table. Equally . . .

MOHAN: That's more than I got before.

ROMILA: I'll go for it. I could use the money for the baby.

DONNY: So who is up for it. Mohan . . . Romila.

MOHAN/ROMILA: (*Together*) Me.

They frustrate each other by overlapping.

(*Together*) . . . *Me*

DONNY: Who?

Again they overlap.

BOTH: Me

Frustration, Pause.

ROMILA: Me.

MOHAN: Me.

ROMILA: I'll take it for 25 cents less.

MOHAN: And I for 50 cents less.

SHYAMALA: 25 cent more is already down to 50 cents under.

The scene is slowly becoming a bidding game.

DONNY: Only 200 jobs . . . your turn Romila.
ROMILA: 60 cents less.
DONNY: Mohan your bid.
MOHAN: 61 cents.
DONNY: Who is going lower?
MOHAN/ROMILA: (*Together*) Me.

Pamella steps in.

PAMELLA: No me . . . I'll work for free.
SUSAN: That's as low as anybody can go.

All silent.

DONNY: Pamella dear you spat, split missed my promotion party but I'm glad you're back to your senses.
MOHAN: I knew she was for herself.
ROMILA: True colours show now.
DONNY: Cross the picket line Pamella.

She stays still.

Don't worry about them. I still love you. We'll have fun together. I'll give you allowance from my raise.
PAMELLA: Did you get the raise, for not joining us?
DONNY: You're talking to a foreman.
PAMELLA: Pimp . . . as far as I am concerned.
DONNY: What?
PAMELLA: You dropped a quarter.

Donny looks down.

DONNY: Where?
PAMELLA: (*Kicking imaginary quarter.*) There in the back.

Donny runs and encounters Shyamala . . . she kicks imaginary quarter . . .

SHYAMALA: To your left.

They all give Donny a run around until he finds himself looking for quarter under Pamella's feet. She lifts her feet and there isn't anything.

DONNY: (*Angry, flabbergasted*) You are playing tricks on me.
PAMELLA: You had to be out of your mind if you thought you could beat us with dirty trick of Chamber of Commerce. You couldn't pay me to work for less than equal pay. And when you go back give this to slime ball boss of yours.

Donny returns bruised and clothes torn, back to Sly's office.

SLY: Where are the 200 women you went to hire.
DONNY: They've gotten smart.
SLY: The women?
DONNY: Very smart.
SLY: You've gone nuts.
DONNY: I am telling you.
SLY: You are all bruised . . . who did this to you?
DONNY: Did you know those women are mighty angry.
SLY: Yes.
DONNY: Well I didn't.
SLY: None willing to return?

Donny pathetically nods "No."

Susan . . . Where is she? Must be in the ladies room putting make-up. . . (*Remembers*) Oh shit she's walled off too. This is worst pressure I felt since World War II. Donny bring my anti-depressants.

Donny brings his cheque book, cash, and bonds, Investment certificates.

This has a soothing effect (*He rubs his head on them*) . . . but what's worse is that my bank manager turned out to be a woman—all our money is rotting. I'm afraid I have to negotiate.

DONNY: Does that mean you're going to give in.

SLY: Of course not . . . but I've got to talk. I'm depressed. Call them in.

DONNY: Pamella?

SLY: Your girl friend.

DONNY: She isn't the same anymore?

SLY: Why, does she bite?

DONNY: Does she ever. She gave me this note for you.

Gives note.

SLY: What does it say.

Returns note to Donny and commands him to read.

DONNY: (*Reading*) . . . Our demands . . . Equal pay for equal work . . . drop charges. . . . Rehire unconditionally.

SLY: Doesn't sound like music to my ears!

Snatches the letter from Donny and reads himself.

. . . Right to win . . . justice . . . bla . . . bla . . . bla . . . history of women's wages in Quebec . . . bla . . . bla . . . bla . . . and pay equity in . . . other parts of the country . . .

Sly crushes the letter in his hand and throws it.

I see what you mean. She is a communist turned feminist . . . one of those frustrated types who don't shave their legs.

DONNY: And silly me, I thought I could make her my full time wife.

SLY: Call her in.

DONNY: Don't say I didn't warn you.

Donny steps out addressing women.

The company is ready for negotiation.

The women get ready and Donny gets out. The women walk over to Sly's office.

SLY: (*To Pamella*) Haven't I seen this face before.

He kisses her hand.

PAMELLA: I told you "remember this face."
SLY: Do you still hate me?
PAMELLA: Get to the point Mr. Sly!
SLY: I've got good news for you. I want to hire you back.
PAMELLA: Terms—equal pay.
SLY: In case you read the newspaper . . . (*opens the paper*) finance section . . . here . . . "The plunge in profits has taken toll on charitable programs financed by Sly Textile Corporation. (*To Pamella*) Do you want more charitable programmes suspended? I don't know what a nice girl like you is doing with . . .

Pamella cuts him.

PAMELLA: In case you're serious? The negotiation . . .
SLY: If I wasn't serious I wouldn't have gone out of my way to start this factory.
PAMELLA: And give us bleeding nose, chronic ulcers, swollen ankles, pollution, waste and inflation. But what you forgot is equal wages.
SLY: You're asking me to slash my profits. Well I can't because that sends me into depression. (*Looks at Donny*) Only other way is to cut Donny's wages, who is time and the half bigger than you. Can you see yourself ever being like him.

Donny inflates.

PAMELLA: What's huge isn't great, but keep your pride if it makes you feel strong. All I want is equal pay for equal work.
SLY: How do you expect to get any wages when you are parading

outside and machines are rusting inside.

PAMELLA: We are talking **equal** wages not **any** wages.

SLY: You pretty well know company can't afford that.

PAMELLA: You're not going to fool me again with that line. If the company can afford scabs, the chamber of commerce, then it can pretty well afford equal wages.

SLY: I gave you so much free coffee break, lunch break, dental plan, sick leave, paid vacation and above all secretary's day. But you can't get everything free. Equal pay is out of question. Next you are going to ask divest from South Africa and set up a public inquiry.

PAMELLA: I hate everything you say.

SLY: Then go on hating. What can one expect from a woman who dumps her boyfriend for money and makes everybody pay union dues so that they can get free counselling about their problems with no guaranteed results. Go on parading the streets while your hubbies look after the junior at home.

Sly walks away and holds his head in his two hands.

Donny bring my anti-depressants.

The women step forward clanking pots and pans, raising posters. They directly face the audience.

SHYAMALA: The women have had to fight ever since the world was created.

ROMILA: But history has turned a blind eye to our struggle—as if we were some kind of afternoon tea club.

PAMELLA: We fought the war of independence. We fought the war of liberation. In 1857 we demonstrated against 12 hour work day, low wages, against child labour and horrible working conditions. General strike gripped the town.

SUSAN: But it was no easy task. Women came forward from all over to support us.

SHYAMALA: And scabs were brought loaded in police vans.

ROMILA: And we gave them an earful of our anger.

ALL: Scabs go back. . . . Scabs go back.

PAMELLA: The bosses stood on their balconies and spoke with microphones "who is afraid of bunch of mad women."

SUSAN: That's when our mad courage got madder and we marched ahead to take control of our destiny.

They clank pots and pans and move forward.

SHYAMALA: But the police did what it does best—aimed guns at us. Fired shots in air "back or we shoot."

ROMILA: And people did what they do best—they came chanting support for us "Shoot us."

People come on stage.

PAMELLA: The scabs ran off buried in shame.

SUSAN: Bosses hid their faces in unknown land.

SHYAMALA: And police dropped their guns in disgrace.

ROMILA: And it is for that day you have a 8 hour work day.

PAMELLA: And after that we fought together for minimum wages.

SUSAN: And we fought together for higher wages.

SHYAMALA: And today we are fighting for equal wages.

Mohan steps forward.

MOHAN: Even men have joined in—some employed, some unemployed and some professional activists.

ROMILA: And we'll go all the way.

MOHAN: Their spirit is flying so high that they forget our political leaders have something to say too.

He throws a welcome bow towards the wing and three politicians (like Daryl, Larry and Larry of Newhart TV show) enter. All clap.

POLITICIAN: Hi, I am the Govt. This is my first opposition and this my other opposition.

They wave.

Dear sisters! you have been on strike for months, for a just cause.

SHYAMALA: Is that what you come to tell us?

POLITICIAN: My party takes speical pride in the fact that we have a women's wing in our caucus.

POLITICIAN 2 and 3: Ditto.

POLITICIAN 1: We take pride in women's movement in our country but we don't know what the problem is. Therefore we are an all party fact finding committee.

POLITICIAN 2 and 3: Ditto.

ROMILA: We want equal pay for equal work. Why is it that women remain an underpaid majority in this country.

POLITICIAN 1: This one issue the Govt. and opposition are united. It's the single non-partisan domestic issue on which . . .

POLITICIAN 2 and 3: We all agree.

PAMELLA: That pretty well sums up why there is still 40% wage disparity in the country.

POLITICIAN 1: Talk of equal rights, we have charter of rights today. Talk of suffrage of women, we have voting right today. Talk of affirmative action we have quota system today.

Susan points him to stop.

SUSAN: Spare us the history Daryl, Larry & Larry. We don't want to know from you what we have already won.

SHYAMALA: Tell us what you are going to do about our wages.

POLITICIAN 1: For that you'll have to wait until all party fact finding committee publishes its most updated recommendations.

All wave and exit. The women and all other actresses/actors come on stage. Talk to audience.

SHYAMALA: You know, it has taken men only a few million years to set up a task force, which will come out with the already known findings that women are paid 40% less than men in this country.

ROMILA: And the future recommendation—a national commission which will be made up of unwilling men who undoubtedly will do the unnecessary—recommend another commission.

PAMELLA: We have ministry of women's affairs but our affiars are run by commissions.

SUSAN: Today more women are in work-force as long as they accept lower wages and continue to take care of changing diapers and serving home.

SLY: Don't say we don't care about you. We invented washing machine, vacuum cleaner, microwave and birth control.

SHYAMALA: And you invented inequality because deep down in your heart you expect us to make you feel stronger and not earn equal to you.

DONNY: So what do you want us to do let you climb on top of our head.

PAMELLA: No! It doesn't shatter our ego if we aren't on top. Help us make a world where nobody is below anybody and everybody is equally dependent on everybody.

MOHAN: As soon as you get little chance you start hammering us with your lecture about all female revolution.

SLY: Can't you be a little polite. Even the critique of the play would agree you could have been subtle.

ROMILA: And so they tell us we aren't subtle in our demands.

PAMELLA: But what's subtle about a truck driver earning more than a nurse.

SHYAMALA: And what is subtle about a chairman of C.N. earning more than minister of women's affairs.

ROMILA: And for that matter what is subtle about a male high school drop-out earning more than a female college graduate.

PAMELLA: Do you think it's fair?

If the audience don't scream "No" other actors would.

ALL: No.

SUSAN: But they won't give us equality if we don't fight to take it.

SHYAMALA: So please, if you can, help us fight. We need you.

All Bow.

LAND WHERE THE TREES TALK

"Land Where the Trees Talk" is a play based on Quebec's largest hydro-electric project—the James Bay. Mercury poisoning, a deadly disease, breaks out among the area residents of James Bay after the first phase of the project.

The unborn child of a young unwed Cree woman called Lubna is poisoned by mercury transmitted into her bloodstream through contaminated fish. Lubna visits the spirit of mother earth and the tree only to witness similar disintegration of their fate. Local doctor Karuna Kate joins hand with Cree Chief Greenway and demands a ban until an impartial environmental assessment of the Megawatt-project. While Prime Minister Muldoon is oblivious, Premiere Bonapart is intent on pushing for even bigger project—the "Megawatt II." Final showdown site is the Hydro Quebec headquarters where Chief Greenway, Dr. Kate and their sympathizers are holed in.

The play probes native land rights in the midst of environmental awareness—"are we inheriting the earth from our ancestors or stealing it from our children ?"

Reviews

"Land Where the Trees Talk" is a fast paced, often hilarious overview of Canadian history as it pertains to the treatment meted out to its native people.

"In light of recent events, "Land Where the Trees Talk" is a highly imaginative, timely and devastatingly satiric theatrical achievement. It makes me laugh, even as it makes us think, because behind the laughter and the barbs are hitting home time and time again with deadly accuracy.

" . . . Well integrated piece of theatre that should not be missed."

Myron Galloway
The Suburban

"' . . . Land' has echoes in real-life drama."

Pat Donnelly
The Gazette

" . . . Land Where the Trees Talk is an inspiration, is an imaginative entertaining and most informative 90 minutes that you will spend in a theatre for a long time to come.

This is not a preach-to-you style show where the guilt trip is laid on the audience, but a well thought out and thoroughly enjoyable play."

Roger Peace
The Montreal Downtowner

A note from the playwright

In 1984 in Bhopal, India, the world saw the worst devastation caused by poisonous gases since the world war: 5,000 dead, 80,000 disabled, more than 200,000 injured and uprooted. The ugly face of Union Carbide's corporate criminality continues to unfold with increased infant mortality rate and alarming rise in number of deformed, disabled and still births. Once again, we were told, "that's the price for progress and development."

When a deformed, disabled or dead baby is born due to environmental or industrial damages, it's an infringement of human rights and on justice. Too often, many such "development" projects are possible only because human rights and justice are denied.

The Bhopal incident is not an isolated one. I believe there is similarity between Bhopal and Quebec's plan regarding James Bay hydro project. The James Bay project of Quebec is not only environmentally unsafe, it is an attack on the land rights of native people of the area.

By ramming through James Bay Hydro project, the government of Quebec has denied the native people the right to their land and its resources. While the hydro project has earned dollars to the government of Quebec, it has displaced and uprooted the native people, making them refugees in their own land. Given the lack of political power dispensed to the native people, and given the fact that they are the only direct victims of this project, we are talking about environmental racism.

Canada and Quebec have a lot to be ashamed of in their treatment of the native people. And one needs to scrutinize the link between the environmental disasters and the land rights of the native people.

"Land Where the Trees Talk" is one such attempt.

List of Characters

Earth	Mother earth
Tree	A Tree
Chief	Native chief in 1536
Greenway	Native Chief, Grandfather
Dr. Karuna Cate	Doctor on Reserve, in her mid-thirties
Captain	European explorer (1536)
Patrick	Crew on ship
Claude	Crew on ship
Simone	Crew on ship
Bob Bonaparte	Premier
Thomas	Young native, 22 yrs of age
Lubna	Young native woman, 19 yrs
Robertta Notaway	Industrialist, Advisor
Diox In	Investor, Industrialist
Tox In	Investor, Industrialist
Tracy Thorn	Secretary
Nadilka	Nurse
Mitsumi Talkalot	Reporter
Chorus	Native Indians, Narrator, Policeman, Crowd, Media, Dancers, Blind man, Telegram boy, news-vendor, patients.
Chin Muldoon	Prime Minister

"Land Where the Trees Talk" was first produced by *Teesri Duniya Theatre* at the Centaur Theatre on September 26 for a two week run. The cast and the production team was as follows:

Lubna Springwater	Anita Choudhury
Crew member, Tox In	James Douglas
Crew member, Diox In	Stephen Slavey
Crew member, Roberta Nottaway, Tracy Thorn	Emily Harpp
Captain, Blind Eyewitness, Paitent	Andre Martin
Native woman	Mahatma Talkalot
Prime Minister Muldoon	Jena Martin
Narrator, Premiere Bonaparte, Police officer	Ken McDonough
Tree, Nurse Nadilka	Angela Seth
Thomas, Patient in waiting room, Telegram boy	Jaleel Siddiqui
Mother Earth, Patient in waiting room	Noeleen De Silva
Native Chief (1536), Newspaper vendor	Raminder Singh
Chief Greenway	James Ross Thomson
Dr. Karuna Cate, Police Officer	Nancy Irene Wood

Director	Jack Langedijk
Light Design	Jean Charles Martel
Set design	Lucinda Vandenieuwegiessen
Stage manager	Teressa Kaeser
Music	Catherine Potter (Flute)
Ganesh Anandan	(Mridangam & percussion),
Jamie Irwin	(Guitar)
Production manager	Heather Ritchie
Poster Design	Raminder Singh

LAND WHERE THE TREES TALK

The stage is split level, with the higher floor being appox. seven feet above the lower. The lower stage is set with trees hung with burlap moss. Moss also adorns the walls. Several large rocks are situated stage left, stage right and centre stage. There is a strong smell of incense in the air.

Play opens with a cast member sitting in circle. Cast enters by ones and twos, stating their names and the roles which they are to play. Musicians enter and take positions on top of promenade, stage left. Cast member who plays tree enters. Lights fade out. The cast turn on flashlights one by one. The Tree does a dance symbolizing environmental destruction. Dance ends with chief taking a necklace from the tree. Crowd of explorers standing around tub.

NARRATOR: Stardate 1536, Tuesday, 3:15 pm. They sailed all summer, despite relentless seas, fleas, rats, scurvy and only one Rene Simard 8-track that played over and over and over and over . . . Finally . . .
SIMONE: Halt . . . Land . . .
PAT/CLAUDE: Land . . .
CAPTAIN: Land . . .
ALL: and . . . (Deep Sigh)
PAT/CLAUDE: Can we go home now?
CAPTAIN: Shut up and get me my golf clubs.
SONG: This land was your land and now it's my land . . .

Scene change. Patrick and Claude are seen holding Simone by the legs. She is searching the water for riches. Crowd of natives sitting, stage left.

NARRATOR: 1536, Thursday, 3:16 pm.
CAPTAIN: Have you got those samples I asked for?
CLAUDE: Captain, the tricorder is totally fuc . . .
PATRICK: Not functioning, Captain.
SIMONE: Wait . . . I caught something.
PAT/CLAUDE: Captain . . . she's got something.

Simone brings up squash. Captain comes from golf practice.

CAPTAIN: A squash.
SIMONE: Here is something more. (*Brings up corn*)
PATRICK: Corn!
CLAUDE: Habitant!
SIMONE: Pea soup, and it's already canned.
CAPTAIN: Plenty of food supply here . . . do you think there could be humanoids living round these Isles?
NATIVES: (*Sarcastically*) Nooo!!!
CREW: (*Crew looks at audience surprised*) N-n-nooooo!
SIMONE: It's our land.
CLAUDE/PAT: We found it.
SIMONE: Ow . . . ow . . . ow . . .
PATRICK: What happened?
SIMONE: My hand is stuck. . . . Help me you fool. . . . Pull me . . .
CAPTAIN: Pull her . . . On the count of three . . . 1, 2, 3 . . .

All fall. Simone's hand is covered in crude oil.

SIMONE: Yuck! What's all this black yucky stuff?
CAPTAIN: (*Happily*) That's not black yucky stuff, that's bubbling crude.
PATRICK: Oil, that is?
CAPTAIN: Black gold?
CLAUDE: Texas tea?
SONG: Weeeellll, The first thing you know,
Jean's a millionaire, The french folks said:
"Jean, stay over there",
They said Canada is the place you ought to be,
So they loaded up the ship and moved Chicoutimi . . .

Quebec, that is . . . Distinct Society.

NARRATOR: 1536, 2 Wednesdays later, 3:17 pm. Our intrepid explorers finally confront native life forms for the first time, behind a tree.

A group of natives, circled. Crew is petrified, huddled together, behind a tree.

SIMONE: Jesus Christ, there are more of them!
PATRICK: Must be tonnes of them.
CLAUDE: What ya do . . . weigh them?
CAPTAIN: Shut up! (*Natives Laugh.*) . . . Duck!

Crew drops to ground. . . . Rises up. Natives laugh again.

The savages! Load your guns.

SIMONE: Sounds like a Native war cry. Bunch of animals in animal skins.
CAPTAIN: At least they aren't naked covered in white clay.
CREW: Yeahhhh! *(Disgusted)*
PATRICK: White clay, I hear it's great for the skin.
CLAUDE: And a little cucumber over the eyes . . .
CAPTAIN: Shut up! You know what I think . . . One of us should go and talk to them.

All push Patrick towards natives caught by surprise, Patrick tries to draw native's attention.

PATRICK: So . . . ya wanna buy a watch? How about those Expos? Did you hear the one about. . . . ? (*Natives laugh unaware of Patrick.*) At least they have a sense of humour.

Natives laugh again, unaware. Patrick, scared, runs behind crew.

Put away the gun first.

CAPTAIN: Do what I say!

Natives slowly turn pointing at sky still unaware of explorers.

SIMONE: Oh my God! It's turning! It's coming after us. (*Crew drops to ground.*) We're dead, we're dead, we're dead, we're dead . . .

Natives stand over Simone, curious. Simone shocked/frightened looks up.
Natives highly amused. Simone scampers back to crew.

Oh my God, it's a woman.

They huddle in a line with Captain at the rear.

CAPTAIN: We'd like to talk to someone in charge.
PATRICK: And not in the kitchen.
CREW: A man!

One native mimes 'what's man?' another native gestures phallically all natives laugh.
Captain walks to front of stage. Crew follows.

CAPTAIN: Now I must return and write in my diary of the splendid discovery the land is.
SIMONE: Discovery?
CAPTAIN: Yes, I put them on the map.
PATRICK: Pardon me Captain, the land bears witness to the history of their existence. (*Natives applaud*)
CAPTAIN: Except no civilized man knew about them.
PATRICK: Distance of two oceans, does not mean their history does not forego your expedition. (*Natives applaud again*)
CAPTAIN: History is written of art and culture. The nomadic creatures of the new world are devoid of any culture—they don't even know agriculture—(*Crew laughs*) They are simply a band (*Crew sings: 'Burning down the house'*)—a group of kindred families that claim certain hunting ground and stick together in chase and war. I am the explorer who saw the riches here and that's where the history begins.

Natives and the crew raise their eyes and look at the audience and in unison voice say . . . "oooohhh"!

NARRATOR: Stardate 1537, Monday, 3:20 pm. Now that the men are cured, it was business as usual.

Crew parodies killing the animals as they call out the names.

PATRICK: Bison!
CLAUDE: Wolf.
SIMONE: Buffalo!
PATRICK: Bear.
CLAUDE: Otter!
SIMONE: Beaver!

Chief arrives. While chief talks, natives die in exaggerated slowness, their bodies fall one over the other reaching forward, forming an abstract formation.

CHIEF: I want you to take your cross back. I want you to take back everything you gave our tribes. (*Crew eavesdrops*)

CAPTAIN: You want to call off this beautiful trade relationship we've got.

CHIEF: I am sensing a major catastrophe.

CAPTAIN: Catastrophe? (*To crew*) Get back to work! (*To chief*) I say, the standard of life has gone up.

CHIEF: Look at us. Look at us! The great Iroquois Nation fighting people against people, tribe against tribe.

CAPTAIN: What have I got to do with that?

CHIEF: It never happened before we traded.

CAPTAIN: You traded because you loved it. (*To crew*) Get back to work.

CHIEF: Take it back please. I don't want your comforts.

Chief throws Cross at Captain's feet. Turns and walks stage front with a bundle, which is the blanket shrouded body of her grandson.

CAPTAIN: Your people do. Can you stop them from wanting. Oh no. Oh no, Chief. I gave what your people didn't have and they loved it. They wanted them so much that they began killing each other to obtain them. And all I got from you is medicine when we were sick and maize. So what!

CHIEF: To the long list of gifts, add one more-disease.

CREW: Disease?

Chief unveils the wrapped object. It is the dead body of a young boy. Crew moves slowly to surround dead boy.

CAPTAIN: What's this? Some kind of joke?

CHIEF: This isn't a joke, Captain. This is my grandson.

CREW: Grandson?!

CHIEF: More precisely—his dead body.

CAPTAIN: Sorry . . .What happened?

CHIEF: He came down with a strange illness—rashes, spots all over his body, skin popping out. Any child who came near fell victim to the same illness. Today my whole family is wiped out. And now the whole tribe is struck with the strange illness. I don't want the diseases you brought.

Address crew accusingly.

Why did you come here? What do you want? To explore . . . to find us . . . Well you found us. Now what are you going to do with us? Just go . . . go . . .

Chief frantically pushes against crew. and dies in the last surviving natives's arms. Surviving native takes chief's necklace. Puts it on. Turns to captain.

NATIVE: Go home.

CAPTAIN: This is our home, now.

Native walks and kneels at earth's feet. Surviving native's haunting cries are heard.

CAPTAIN: Get back to work . . . Get back to work . . . Why was she so uptight?

CLAUDE: Her grandson is dead.

CAPTAIN: Why is she blaming me?

SIMONE: Her people are dying.

CAPTAIN: Would anybody explain in plain and simple English.

PATRICK: Epidemic. Disease—when it strikes one person, it wipes out whole town.

SIMONE: Shhhh! Can you hear it?

Crew hear haunting singing from native kneeling at earth.

CLAUDE: I remember when this disease broke out back home. It was awful. My grandmother burnt all the clothes to prevent the spread of germs of disease.

CAPTAIN: Spread of . . . germs? What are you talking about?

CLAUDE: My grandmother suspected, the germs, very tiny,

PATRICK: . . . too small to even see. They carried the disease from one person to another.

CLAUDE: All it takes is simple contact. Like when Simon sneezes near us, we all get a runny nose.

SIMONE: I think we brought our germs through our blankets and scarfs.

CAPTAIN: (*Loud laugh*) That's funny. Invisible germs. I thought I brought men with me. And how ferociously the savages fought against my men resisting the cross. Now you tell me they can't resist what you suspect to be a tiny germ.

CLAUDE: The natives have no resistance.

CAPTAIN: And all these days I thought, the most formidable adversary of man was the man eating predator.

SIMONE: Who would have thought that our contact will bring disease to the savages?

CAPTAIN: And who'd have thought we could conquer without war.

PATRICK: What do you mean?

CAPTAIN: If the 'germs' had minds at all, there would be little doubt in those minds that it was they who made the final conquest happen. This planet is up for the taking now. (*Pause*) Final conquest.

PATRICK: Must we make disease a medium of conquest?

The crew forms a tableau representing a hug of humanity.

CAPTAIN: I will stop at nothing for the patriotism I owe to the motherland. Indeed the conquest is made by those who are crazy and those who dare. I am both.

Narrator recites dates as if the pages of a calendar were turning. One by one, actors move forward to face audience.

1608: First permanent settlement in Quebec, Champlain arrives.
1650: 50-90% native population killed in first century of contact.
1660: My cousin Mary and Winofred were tried for witchcraft in Connecticut, they were acquitted.
1700: 50% Inca population killed by smallpox.
1750: French Revolution.
1760: My great great grandfather was born in Poland.
1780: A little girl and 368 other treehugger were cut alive by the Maharaha.
1800: 2 million tribal people wiped out working in mines. African slaves brought in to replace them.
1810: My great grandmother came over from Ireland and yes she was white.
1820: Church splits. Rise of Protestants.
1867: Canadian Confederation.

Natives surround speaker, vying to sign land treaties.

I got a lake in the North, a hill in the west etc. Great Lakes.

Freeze, then actors once again move forward to face audience.

1918:1226 signed land treaties with the Natives are violated.
1919: WWI 90, 000 dead 130, 000 injured.
Nobel prize winner Haber discovers poison gas and says 'poison gas is higher form of killer.'
Russian revolution.
1935: West Virginia 30, 000 die of silicosis.
1938: 1 million Armenians, 6 million Jews, 14 million Russians, mas-

sacred.

1945: Manhattan Project, Hiroshima. Industry produces 3.5 tons of T.N.T. per person.

1950: U.S. produces 150 million Anophiles per month the most potent Malaria causing mosquito.

1982: Chernobyl, Three-Mile Island.

1983: AIDS

1984: City in Mexico 1500 dead, 700 injured by explosion of PIMEX Oil.

1987: Industry produce 3 kilos pesticide\person 1 million suffer pesticide poisoning.

1989: Lead contamination in Western Canada.

1990: Deforestation, global warming, acid rain, P.C.B. scares.

Narrator ceases dates. Individual cast members recite a personal event and exit. Premier Bonaparte standing stage front. Robertta Notaway standing behind a chair stage right. Duo enter stage left.

DIOX: Stardate 1990, Tuesday, 3:22 pm.

TOX: A contemporary politician's office . . .

TOX: And his trusty servant, top chief executive, land speculator, financial consultant, industrial specialist.

ROBERTTA: Land pimp.

DIOX/TOX: Robertta Notaway.

DIOX: And us . . . we're the In brothers Diox and Tox. And now for the big cheese . . . Premier Bonaparte.

BONAPARTE: Take a seat. The world starts here . . .

OTHERS: Your office? Up North? Kingston?

BONAPARTE: No, It's a nation builder project . . .

OTHERS: Bill 101? A strip joint? Mcdonald's!!!

BONAPARTE: It should rid us from economic misery.

DIOX/TOX/ROB: Mummy, 101, G.S.T.

BONAPARTE: The James Bay Project.

DIOX/TOX/ROB: Megawatt !!!!!!!! (*Looks out to audience*)

BONAPARTE: Most politicians write their autobiography after they retire.

DIOX: Politician?

TOX: Politician.

BONAPARTE: Look it up. But seeing the whole new world coming to birth, I might write my autobiography even before I retire.

DIOX: (*Turning frantically the pages of a dictionary*) Prophylactic, potatoes, priests. Politician . . . ah . . . one interested or engaged in politics, especially as a profession, see prostitute.

ROBERTTA: 200 dams and dikes, half a million ton of concrete, 200 million cubic meters of reservoir, 1500 km long road, bar, airport, investors from all over the world.

DIOX: People are waking up.

TOX: Building rents going up by the minute.

DIOX: Hotels and tourism booming.

TOX: Plus 10000 new jobs.

BONAPARTE: There is more.

DIOX(*To Tox*): Where?

TOX: Here.

DIOX: (*Confused*) Now?

TOX: (*Diox emotionally crushed*) Shaadd aaap.

BONAPARTE: Just a few years ago it was virgin territory with just a few trappers and hunters. Today, it produces 10,000 megawatt hydro-power.

DIOX: And don't forget magnesium.

TOX: Aluminum.

DIOX: Pulp and paper

TOX: All conveniently located.

SONG: Down by the riverside,
Down by the riverside,
Down by the riverside.
That's where we like to dump, da dump.

All jump into air.

BONAPARTE: We're in this together, ladies and gentlemen. In the common spirit, common interest, vision and dollar work together.

ALL: Together. All for us and none for them.

ROBERTTA: Doesn't look like you're going to have problems writing your speech. You've touched life.

Robertta kisses Bonaparte on cheek, Tox follows suit, Diox aims for Bob, misses, and gets Tox. Tox not amused.

BONAPARTE: That's what I am worried about.

All cringe in fright. Glancing at sky for unseen danger.

ROBERTTA: What do you mean?
DIOX: What does he mean?
BONAPARTE: How many lives has the Megawatt touched.
ROBERTTA: A few Indians, I think.
DIOX: A couple of Caribou.
TOX: A field mouse or two.
BONAPARTE: Everybody today talks about environmental consequences.
ROBERTTA: You mean, how many lives have been affected by environmental consequences?
DIOX: Of course there are those who perpetuate falsehood.
TOX: But nothing is true
DIOX: (*To Tox*) . . . Or false
TOX: Until it's proven.
BONAPARTE: There is pressure for review.
DIOX: (*To Tox*) And review boards are filled with young blood.
TOX: Who work to perpetuate fear.
ROBERTTA: That's why I prefer my own review. Because theirs does not give the facts. The facts are right here, in James Bay. Just a decade ago there was a jungle here. Now we have running water, sewage treatment and power lines. So my dear Bonaparte premier, as a team, we will brave all reviews.
BONAPARTE: I must work to create a strong administrative body.

Bonaparte grabs hair of Diox and Robertta and Yanks.

And just to make them think I'm doing it for them, I'll plaster the smiling faces of native children on all the street corners and in all parts of the country. Now get those bulldozers dozing, those saws sawing, dumptrucks dumping. Get to work!

Music. All actors enter dancing covering whole stage. One native carrying sign, raises it. The sign says: "A Peaceful Native Village". Robertta, Tox, Diox singing megawatt rap and on the beat push na-

tives into corner, taking their land away.

CHORUS 1: A peaceful little village somewhere outside of James Bay.

Diox, Tox, Rob sing rap.

RAP-SONG: Let me tell you a story about Megawatt,
It's a big bucks project we love a lot, Hunh, hunh.
Megawatt, Megawatt, rah, rah, rah,
If you're really good we'll give some stock to you
Hunh, hunh.
I said M-E-G-A-W-A and a double yah, a double Tee
It's the biggest money maker for the movers and the shakers in all of history. Hunh.

CHORUS 1: What happened to our land?
CHORUS 2: It's all flooded here.
CHORUS 3: The trees.
CHORUS 4: So they are at work again.
CHORUS 2: Who are they?
CHORUS 4: Who do you think they are?
CHORUS 5: These cigarette butts and beer cans. They aren't from around here.
CHORUS 3: So that explains why heavy machinery was piled along the icy road throughout the winter.
CHORUS 6: And as soon as the ice melts—there starts bulldozing.
CHORUS 2: And before anybody could get their act together, they have eaten another piece of our land.
CHORUS 4: Bastards . . . Let them come this time.
ROBERTTA: How.
CHORUS 2: It's you again.
ROBERTTA: Our man in politics saw the light and lights are green for the world's largest
DIOX/TOX/ROB: The Megawatt Project!!!!!!
CHORUS 2: How come no one ever consults us?
ROBERTTA: Because our man in politics knows what is best.
DIOX: He does.
TOX: He really does.

CHORUS 4: Oh yeah . . . 'Trust us. He knows what's best.' Well no more. You will destroy our land no more. We've got injunctions from the superior court. (*Shows the injunction.*) Preserve it in your files.

ROBERTTA: Good move little lady—but my 500 dollar an hour plus 3 times a year paid vacation lawyer got your injunction overturned just in 4 days in court of appeals. And if you think I don't know much—the Supreme Court of Canada refused to hear a challenge to the ruling. (*Flashes verdict*) Frame it in your living room.

CHORUS 4: We'll try in the Native court. (*Diox/Tox/Rob laugh*)

Do an insulting Indian dance. Natives not impressed.

ROBERTTA: Just kidding. Lighten up. It was funny in Chateauguay. Right. Get this. Defendants—Megawatt.

Throws a punch into air. Natives cringe.

Government of Quebec,

Punch and cringe.

Government of Canada.

Another punch and one more cringe.

But sorry little lady, so far you don't even have the right to vote.

Robertta knocks natives over with a hip check.

So let me read it to you . . . Once upon a time . . . Da . . . da . . . da . . . therefore it is hereby notified under . . . da . . . da . . . da . . . that inhabitants of the said land . . . da . . . da . . . da . . . must end the occupation immediately . . . da . . . da . . . da . . . failing which the matter should be handed over to the proper authorities . . . da . . . da . . . da . . . rules proper compensation be given to the affected.

CHORUS 6: (*Slowly rising*) Compensation? What gives them the right to decide our compensation?

ROBERTTA: Ask them. But if I were you who thought Megawatt is a loss, I'd pocket the compensation and cut my losses. Megawatt will be here forever. Long after you're dead. (*Walking away*) Get those bulldozers dozing, dumptrucks dumping. . . . Let's go!

Natives form a human wall to the drumbeat. The two opposing lines confront one another. At the end of the confrontation the Diox/Tox/Rob falls to ground.

ROBERTTA: Here they go again. Another road block.

CHORUS 4: You got your mind blocked, otherwise you'd realize the environmental consequences.

ROBERTTA: And if you had a mind you'd get the hell out of here.

CHORUS 4 : Who the hell do you think you are?

CHORUS 6: What do you think? A piece of paper will change the history.

Policeman arrives.

POLICEMAN: Hold it. Police! What's going on here! What's going on here?

One native steps forward from barricade and is shot dead.

CHORUS 2: Look officer . . .

POLICEMAN: (*Fires shot at Chorus 2*) Bang!!!!! You're dead!!!

Falls down dead.

CHORUS 6: You just shot an unarmed innocent woman.

CHORUS 2: (Chorus 2 Gets Up) I'm OK . . . I'm OK . . .

CHORUS 6: He just shot you point blank through the heart.

CHORUS 4: I know he shot me, but look, we have no time to deal with this issue right now.

ALL: Oh yeah!

Scene starts prior to police entry.

CHORUS 6: What do you think? A piece of paper will change the history.

Policeman arrives again.

POLICEMAN: What's going on here? Don't you guys realize you're blocking this road illegally.

CHORUS 3: Bullshit. What do you think you're doing . . acting in a John Wayne movie?

POLICE: John Wayne . . . One more word like that and you have had it.

CHORUS 3: Excuse me officer.

POLICE: Shut up.

CHORUS 3: We belong here. You can take the land from us, but you cannot take us from the land.

TOX: (*Mimics native*) 'Cannot take us from the land.'

DIOX/TOX/ROB: (*To audience*) Here they go getting all emotional again.

POLICE: Shut up.

CHORUS 2: We got jurisdiction, officer. Doesn't that count for anything.

POLICE: Shut up . . . Look, this matter will be taken care of in the courts. I don't want to see any of you around here any more. Break it up. Break it up.

All protest, form group, but are dispersed. Earth enters into group in guise of Baglady pulling shopping cart. Group spins and follows Baglady to stage front chanting anti-eco slogans. Fade into street scene with Baglady raving.

EARTH: But, I am the Earth, the mother. Today, I am struck by men of greed and with myopic visions. They gather in their corporate rooms, in pious garbs and recruit the innocent and command strike. Like Maniacs they do. They manipulate the flow of the river with bulldozers and backhoes, drowning tonnes of rocks and soil where from time immemorial the beaver had ruled. Don't you realize that taking the earth away won't leave anything—not even for your own children. So you think rivers can wash away your industrial sins.Why don't you listen. I'm your mother, Earth. Step on a crack, break your Mother's back. Step on a crack, break your mother's back.

CHORUS: Step on a crack! (*Whispers*)

BONAPARTE: Problems, problems, problems. Now, you can give us this here land or we can come on in and take it. What's yer answer, Injun? That's not the answer I was lookin' for. We come in peace. Talk big land deal. Good for us. Good for you. Everybody wins. What ya say? Ah, come on. Just a smidgen, a dot . . . a sliver. You won't even miss it. Promise. Look, guys, I've already signed the sales agreement.

Cast members run on stage from sidelines to form an unemployment line behind Bonaparte. Thomas in front of line. Bonaparte hands him envelope. All exit but Thomas who reads letter excitedly. Lubna enters.

THOMAS: All right!

LUBNA: Thomas.

THOMAS: Lubna, come here quick.

LUBNA: I'm so glad I found you. Listen, I have to speak to your Grandfather. Where is he?

THOMAS: Wait till you hear what happened. It's really exciting.

LUBNA: Megawatt?

THOMAS: And that's where I'm going to work. I got it!! Well, say something.

LUBNA: Does this mean you won't be travelling the Pow-Wow trail this summer?

THOMAS: Pow-Wow trail? Lubna come on. Lubna it's a job, man. I've been waiting for this a long time. Come on Lubna. You know what this means for us. Remember the time you applied for that job in the bar. . . . Who got it? Lubna, the Indian? No. It was either Maria the Italian, Holly the Irish girl or Marie France the French Canadian. It's never us. We're always the last ones. We always get the short end of the stick. Now we finally have an opportunity to move up, and I am not going to miss it for some Bongos on a Pow-Wow trail.

LUBNA: It's not Bongos. It's drum.

THOMAS: Sorry. Lubna, this is our chance. We can get out of here. We could move somewhere far, to the city. Have our own home.

LUBNA: That's what you said last year.

THOMAS: And that's what I say again because now, we've got this.

LUBNA: This is going to make your grandfather very angry. He's already upset because of too many of us leaving.

THOMAS: And I am upset because he still lives 400 years in the past. I don't have my grandfather's skills hunting invisible seals. That's why I've got to learn new skills to survive in 1990 and Megawatt is my chance.

LUBNA: Count me out from that.

THOMAS: What the hell is that supposed to mean.

LUBNA: I'd rather stay here.

THOMAS: What's the matter with everybody. What? Is it a crime to have a job now?

LUBNA: Shut up!

GREENWAY: Hey! What's going on? What's this war I can hear from across the street. Thomas . . . Lubna . . . ? Thomas . . . a job . . . Megawatt . . . (*To Lubna*) And you approve of this.

LUBNA: Of course, I don't approve of this.

GREENWAY: Good, good!

THOMAS: It's a war all right. It's the war of the two of you against me, who won't understand that we ought to have a chance. A chance that was denied to your generation. But now I have that chance and tell me what's wrong with that.

GREENWAY: It's not wrong or right. It's the death of our people.

THOMAS: That's a mental block that you've got, both of you. You never forget that you are an Indian, and neither do I.

GREENWAY: That's good.

THOMAS: The difference is that I don't want to throw away the chance to make a social change for Indian people.

LUBNA: Social change?

GREENWAY: Don't you understand? That's why they push us into the reserves. Then, come a few years later, they push us out of the reserves. Today, we are just the new niggers around here. Thomas, you are young. But old enough to understand . . .

THOMAS: Thanks, Granddad. I am old enough. I'm glad you acknowledge that.

GREENWAY: Then you should know that every time the white man has come to Indians, it's to take something.

THOMAS: That's why they brought megawatt?

GREENWAY: Yes.

THOMAS: Yes, they may be paying their workers more than us . . .

GREENWAY: Lots more.

THOMAS: That is because they've got skills we haven't got.

GREENWAY: We can learn.

THOMAS: When!!? That's what I'm doing. Don't you see? Look, we've got to play our cards right. We have to join their world because that's the world of progress. We have to do what they do, but do it better. Don't you see that?

GREENWAY: They have been slowly terminating us? You want to do that better than them?

THOMAS: And that's the fear you've fed me since I was born. I am expected to inherit your value system . . . that does not make money . . . value system that's 400 years old in the 21st century.

GREENWAY: It's the 21st century that has got to your grandmother. How can I forget that? How can you forget that? She lies in her grave today because she ate too many fish from the 21st century lake, and today uncle Matthew is in the hospital.

THOMAS: Uncle Matthew should be in Alcoholic's Anonymous.

LUBNA: Thomas . . . think about what you're saying.

GREENWAY: Let him say what he wants. He'll never understand, that bottle, is an escape.

THOMAS: And when he can't find his bottle, he escapes to shoe-polish, shaving lotion and . . .

LUBNA: Thomas . . . mind your . . .

THOMAS: . . . gasoline.

GREENWAY: That's how grim the situation is for him and many others. We are seduced by their vision of glamorous life. And all we get is despair, neglect and unemployment, only because we've got no say in our lives.

THOMAS: That's the standard excuse.

GREENWAY: Oh really. Nobody blames a bunch of Russian workers when they become alcoholics. But who gives a damn about a bunch of drunken Indians.

THOMAS: Look, my only point is that we should work for self-improvement. Now, if you'll excuse me, I've got to see my employer at noon.

LUBNA: Thomas, I think you should visit Uncle Matthew in the hospital.

THOMAS: Look, I'll be late.

GREENWAY: He has severe poisoning. He may not return home.

LUBNA: Really?

THOMAS: I am sorry. I got a bit carried away. Before I go to the work site, I'll visit Uncle Matthew.

GREENWAY: Well, I am glad to see we still have a place in your life.

LUBNA: Grandfather, can I talk to you?

GREENWAY: I'll be at the hospital. Goodbye.

Greenway exits. Couples enter.

THOMAS: You have some teachings for me too.

LUBNA: I'm just confused, by the way you think.

THOMAS: C'mon Lub . . . I'm doing it all for us . . . Let's quit fighting and go dancing. (*Lubna stumbles*) What's the matter?

LUBNA: I don't know . . . but I've been tripping lately. That's why I came to talk to your grandfather.

THOMAS: The witch doctor. . . . What's wrong?

LUBNA: Nothing. Let's go.

Business Diox/Tox/Rob leave. Couples hug, then walk across stage, obviously seriously ill. Scene transforms into Dr. Karuna Cate's hospital waiting room. Lubna already waiting.

NADILKA: Are you going to the party?

LUBNA: Yeah.

Karuna enters.

KARUNA: Who's is that?

NADILKA: It's Lubna Springwater's results.

LUBNA: Hi doctor.

KARUNA: How are you, Lubna?

LUBNA: You're the doctor. You tell me. How am I?

KARUNA: Come into my office.

LUBNA: No, tell me now.

KARUNA: You are . . .

LUBNA: Pregnant?

KARUNA: Is there a problem?

LUBNA: No, no, there's no problem. Thank you, doctor.

KARUNA: No wait, Lubna. I have some questions to ask you. When did you take your last blood test? 6 months, 1 year, more?

LUBNA: Why?

KARUNA: I see unusually high levels of mercury in your blood.

LUBNA: Oh!

KARUNA: I would be curious to see how it was a year ago. More or less or maybe not at all.

LUBNA: I don't know. A year ago, there wasn't a hospital here. Is it serious, doctor?

KARUNA: Come into my office.

Karuna and Lubna exit.

PATIENT 3: (*Coughing disgustingly*) He said, "Would you mind exchanging seats."

Karuna enters with Lubna.

KARUNA: Lubna, I must monitor you regularly. And you might have to go to the hospital in Montreal. Don't worry, it's easy to treat a disease and harder to treat the cause. We'll do our best.

NADILKA: Bye, Lubna. What's wrong, doctor?

KARUNA: Nothing. . . . Have you got the results? . . .

PATIENT: Doctor, I'm next.

NADILKA: Please come here, Mr. Johnson.

KARUNA: We don't need to go in, I have your results right here. Nadilka, take some blood and a small amount of hair just to be sure. Go into the backroom, please and we'll take the samples now.

NADILKA: Oh, these just came in, the final results on the hair from the grade one students.

KARUNA: Are you sure these are right?

NADILKA: Yes.

Greenway enters.

GREENWAY: Are you enjoying your job, doctor.
KARUNA: Yes. Next!
GREENWAY: I said, are you enjoying your job.
KARUNA: And I said, yes.
GREENWAY: Here?
KARUNA: Yes, it's a challenge. Next please.
GREENWAY: Why do we come here?
KARUNA: All I know is that nobody here comes for the common diseases. You'll have to excuse me. I have patients to see.
GREENWAY: Just add one more uncommon one . . .
KARUNA: Nadilka . . .
NADILKA: Sir, you'll have to . . . Chief Greenway!
GREENWAY: Nadilka. . . . A 15 year old boy drowned last week. An Indian boy. The police recovered the body today.
NADILKA: Little Tommy?

Chorus whispers 'Tommy?' 'little Tommy' etc.

KARUNA: Drownings? I thought you people would be born swimmers.
GREENWAY: As far as the elders remember, there haven't been any. But ever since Megawatt and the floods it caused, there have been several.
KARUNA: What are you doing here? Why don't we continue this in my office.
CHORUS: No!
KARUNA: Fine. I didn't say anything before because I didn't want to cause a panic in the community. I have been noticing some patients showing unexpectedly . . .
GREENWAY: . . . high levels of mercury in our blood.
CHORUS: It's in our blood?
KARUNA: Yes, take a look at these. I don't think these are isolated cases. I found that every 2 patients out of 3, who live at the mouth of the river and derive their fish diet from it, are showing signs of mercury poisoning. I have a chemist friend who analyzed the flooded reservoir water. He hasn't confirmed it yet, but I sus-

pect that the flooding released bacteria, which was fed by the decomposing organic matter . . .

GREENWAY: We eat the fish and it kills us.

PATIENT 3: It's in the fish!

CHORUS: In the fish?

KARUNA: Yes.

GREENWAY: Thank you, doctor. Very scientific, doctor, but, it's a repeating story. Each time someone does a blood test, he finds a new type of poison in our blood. (*Chorus whispers poison*) Scientists talk in terms of statistical numbers and authorities invalidate the findings by proving it insignificant. But . . . here, look, you're a statistic. This proves it. But . . . numbers are just numbers. My people have known the fear behind those numbers.

PATIENT 3: Yeah, that's what happened to Lapierre . . .

Chorus whispers names of people they know who have died.

GREENWAY: Who knows how many others have died before their time.

KARUNA: But what do other doctors say?

GREENWAY: What do the politicians say?

CHORUS: Yeah!!

KARUNA: That's silly. Now that the effects of poisoning are well established, there will be public action.

GREENWAY: There is. The politicians square off publicly, blaming each other like this is just another "Just for Laughs" festival.

KARUNA: Is that what you came for? To give me one of your anti-establishment stories. We have the proof and we are going to put the matter right.

GREENWAY: By doing what? Writing another report and sending it off to the government? Where it gets passed from one bureaucrat to another. They aren't human, you know. You rip open a bureaucrat and what do you find, red tape. Do you believe they'll stop Megawatt?

CHORUS: Will they?

KARUNA: It doesn't need to be stopped. I want them to correct the wrong. My work is scientific and is supported by other scientific work.

GREENWAY: What's at stake here, doctor, is more than your scientific work. What's at stake here is the greed of politicians and their disregard for my people.

KARUNA: I'm not a politician, I'm a doctor and I've got work to do. Now, get out.

GREENWAY: It's curious how little you know about what's going on in you own country.

KARUNA: Please don't tell me what I know or don't know. That's the proof of what I know.

GREENWAY: And the white man always have their numbers You see, you're a number. Look at that. What number are you. G30 . . . B29 . . . I7 . . . Bingo.

KARUNA: Oh, shut up!!!! I'm sorry.

GREENWAY: We need someone who they will listen to . . . to tell them what it is they are doing. . . . They are killing my people. But, sometimes, I wonder what the difference between a doctor and a politician really is.

Greenway leaves.

NADILKA: What can we do, doctor?

Scene ends with Karuna and Nadilka kneeling on floor. Music cue. Actors dance across stage. Dance ends. Actors fall to floor except the tree. Lubna is seen hugging tree. Earth enters.

EARTH: How come they don't see me?
LUBNA: What ?
EARTH: I'm real am I not?
LUBNA: What do you want?
EARTH: Can you touch me?
LUBNA: Here, take this—it's all the money I have.
EARTH: Do you use this to feed your children. So pretty and so shiny. (*Screams and throws money down*) I know I'm supposed to scream, but I can't. I can't feed my children. What do you do ?

Lubna exits.

Wait, help me —don't go! . . .

Turns to tree.

I know you'll talk to me. Where's the colonel? Who's Wendy? Does she like Harvey? Where's Mr. McDonald?

Song begins. Actors rise up in pairs, singing.

In the chalet! With the King, . . . Mr. Exxon!!
SONG: (All) Hang down your chin Muldoony,
Hang down your chin and cry.
Hang down your chin Muldoony,
this country's going to die.
Hiding behind a Bush now.
Free Trade is going to fly.
Everyone gagged on 101,
Parizeau helps us die.

Earth exits. Scene changes to ministers office. Secretary is on the phone. Native Diox/Tox/Rob enters.

TRACY: Good morning, minister's office, please hold.
NADILKA: Good morning, I, on behalf of them, would like to see the right honourable minister.
TRACY: Have you got an appointment?
NADILKA: We have been trying for weeks. . . . Lines are always busy.
TRACY: What?
NADILKA: We have been trying for over 400 years.

Tracy back on phone.

TRACY: Sorry to keep you waiting. Can I help you . . . Uh . . . uh . . . un . . . No . . . No . . . (*to lover*) Mommy's very angry with you! She's going to come home and beat you with a big, black whip. . . . One time, two time etc. (*Other call*) Hello, A petition? One minute . . . (*Stomps foot near phone*) Sorry, we seem to be having some construction going on. Please call back another year. un . . . un . . . You are quite welcome. . . . Have a good day. . . . Bye now. (*Puts down the phone . . . To Nadilka*) So would you care for an appointment?

NADILKA: No . . . I would prefer to see him now . . . it's going to take only a few minutes.

TRACY: He doesn't see anyone without an appointment.

NADILKA: We just want to give him this report.

TRACY: The minister is a very busy man.

Chorus screams, parodies a rock star scene. Minister Bonaparte barges in with Diox and Tox. The three of them wearing sunglasses. They use natives as revolving doors, knocking them down in the process.

TRACY: These people would like to . . .

Nadilka crawls ahead to hand a report to Bonaparte.

NADILKA: We want to present you this report . . . and would like you to consider it.

BONAPARTE: (*Glancing at report)* Ah . . . very nice staples. Even margins. Wow! Pass the buck.

Report is passed amongst the Diox/Tox/Rob.

NADILKA: But sir . . .

BONAPARTE: Where's the red tape!

KARUNA: Mr. Bonaparte.

BONAPARTE: That's me.

KARUNA: It's very important.

BONAPARTE: It is?

KARUNA: Dr. Karuna Cate.

BONAPARTE: Hi!

KARUNA: This matter deserves your unqualified attention.

BONAPARTE: It does.

KARUNA: Yes. Many lives are at stake.

BONAPARTE: There are? What the hell is she talking about?

DIOX/TOX/ROB: Megawatt!

KARUNA: A major catastrophe. Mercury poisoning and God knows how many other poisons from smelters.

BONAPARTE: Dr. Karuna Cate, as a politician, I've been through the 60s radicalism and now I am seeing a new kind of radicalism called environmentalism. Glad to see our medical professionals getting involved.

DIOX/TOX/ROB: Way to go, Bravo, good girl.

KARUNA: I believe you had time to see my report.

BONAPARTE: Quite frankly . . . no. But I've heard something of the sort. And I am of the opinion that the situation is not as grave as you suggest.

KARUNA: I quite agree with you. It's worse. There have been deaths, especially native people and that should spark some action.

BONAPARTE: When it comes to native people, I have reservations. (*Diox/Tox/Rob chuckle*)

KARUNA: Did I hear you right?

ROBERTTA: Yes, you heard him right. Methyl mercury is not killing anyone. Methyl mercury is a natural phenomenon. Besides, it will die down over time. 10 years, perhaps 15 years, or maybe even 20 years.

DIOX: Besides, not all the fish are contaminated.

TOX: Not all the reservoirs are polluted.

KARUNA: Knowing the industries' record, I'm not surprised by you, but Mr. Minister, is that the official line?

DIOX: The official line is that they should stop eating fish.

TOX: Why do they eat fish when they know it's killing them?

DIOX: There's chicken.

TOX: There's beef.

DIOX: There's hog.

TOX: There's pasta.

DIOX/TOX/ROB: Yeah!

Scene shifts to Thomas and Lubna.

LUBNA: No!

THOMAS: Will you just come back in. They're just having fun.

LUBNA: I'm not going back into that party. I just don't like those uptight, superficial, out of town distinct friends of yours, who actually believe there is something distinct about them. Bunch of loose drunks fly all the way from Montreal and have no decency to learn a word of Cree. And then they have the gall to push French down our throat. And next thing, he pukes all over me. How distinct.

THOMAS: Sometimes, I'd like to see you forget you're Indian and think about things other than your culture and saving the planet.

LUBNA: I'd like to but I can't. We are talking about extinction, Thomas. You can't work for Megawatt, goodnight.

CHORUS: Tell him. Tell him.

LUBNA: I have something to tell you.

Scene shifts. Back to office.

BONAPARTE: Dr. Karuna Cate, my government has promptly advised child bearing women to stop the consumption of fish.

ROBERTTA: We have sent the advice to everybody in green envelopes with government seals on them. (*Ping*) Abstinence is the best cure.

TOX: Dr. Karuna, Megawatt is not an Olympic Stadium.

DIOX: Billions of dollars have gone into it . . .

DIOX/TOX/ROB: And there's no going back.

ROBERTTA: Doctor, we live in a society where people have got to make a choice at every step of their lives.

DIOX/TOX/ROB: They do. . . . They do. . . .

ROBERTTA: The residents of the Megawatt region had a choice.

DIOX/TOX/ROB: They did, they did.

ROBERTTA: Either starve to death or adapt to the monetary modern society and have a fighting chance.

DIOX/TOX/ROB : A chance, a fighting chance.

ROBERTTA: Let me tell you,

DIOX/TOX/ROB: Tell her, tell her, tell her.

ROBERTTA: They didn't have running water, sewage treatment, electricity, school or a community centre on his land before Megawatt.

KARUNA: Big deal. The rest of the country had it all along. Aren't you ashamed of bragging about granting them something so basic, so late.

BONAPARTE: At least they have them. They have jobs . . . good jobs.

DIOX/TOX/ROB: Good jobs, great jobs.

ROBERTTA : They do.

BONAPARTE: Of course if you yank them back to nomadic society, people could sweep streets with brooms and that is also called a job, but we should not and will not because that does not make economical sense.

DIOX/TOX/ROB: Yeah, bravo, bravo, best speech yet.

KARUNA: But environmental destruction does not make economical sense, neither does poisoning.

GREENWAY: Asshole!

DIOX/TOX/ROB: (*Cover ears*) Bad word, bad word, bad word!

GREENWAY: People are dying, you should know that.

ROBERTTA: On the way to progress, we have to suffer some casualties. That's the price we have got to pay. Progress does mean inconvenience sometimes.

TOX: A little.

DIOX: A bit.

GREENWAY: I think it's time you suffer some inconvenience for a change. I'm sorry, Doctor, but let me talk.

BONAPARTE: You mean political deadlock between Ottawa and us?

GREENWAY: Yes! What are you afraid of ?

BONAPARTE: We refuse to succumb to their time-table. It has to be a time table according to the engineers of Megawatt. (*Diox/Tox/Rob yell yeah*)

GREENWAY: And since both of you cannot come to a time table, you serve both as judge and jury, while smelters keep dumping and reservoirs keep poisoning, and you ram through any project specially when the only direct victims are natives. That's 'environmental racism.' (*Good guys yell yeah*)

BONAPARTE: We do not discriminate.

GREENWAY: Neither does pollution. The genocide continues.

BONAPARTE: (*Leans over to talk to Diox/Tox/Rob*) It's hard to talk to people who are more emotional than real.

ROBERTTA: All that talk of genocide and Armageddon looming over us. . . . Makes me real mad.

DIOX: When I hear that rubbish, I don't get angry.
TOX: Instead, I turn to the holy scriptures,
DIOX: To the words of the lord.
TOX: Father forgive them.
DIOX: For they do not know what . . .
TOX: They are talking about.
KARUNA: Oh this is fucking insane!
BONAPARTE: Frankly, we're wasting time. This issue should be addressed Federally. This is Brian's case and you're Brian's race.

Diox/Tox/Rob throw natives off stage. Then Diox/Tox/Rob exit and re-enter on upper stage.
Scene shifts to Thomas and Lubna.

THOMAS: What is it?
LUBNA: It's bad.
THOMAS: What?
LUBNA: It's bad what happened.
THOMAS: What are you talking about?
LUBNA: Think.
THOMAS: Tell me.
LUBNA: I am 4 months pregnant.
THOMAS: You're what?
LUBNA: Dr. Karuna confirmed. . . . I'm going to have a baby.
THOMAS: That's impossible, you can't be.
LUBNA: Maybe for you. But I have 2X chromosomes.
THOMAS: How did it happen?
LUBNA: You know how it happened. You want me to demonstrate.
THOMAS : BUT. . . we used a condom.
LUBNA: The rubber didn't work after all.
THOMAS: What am I going to do?
LUBNA: What are we going to do?
THOMAS : I am not ready to be a father. I'm only 22.
LUBNA: I am only 19.
THOMAS: Oh shit.
LUBNA: Should we talk marriage?
THOMAS: Now you want me to be a husband too?
LUBNA: You don't expect me to be an unwed mother who is bur-

dened on her mother who already has 8 of her own plus an unemployed husband.

THOMAS: What am I . . . What am I? I just started a new job and I'm going to be a father. That's great . . yeah . . . great . . . yes . . . I'll work harder for my son or daughter. I am going to be very serious.

Scene shifts to natives who walks across stage with cringed bodies.

NATIVES: Lions and tigers and bears. (3 x)
MacDonald, Laurier and King oh my.
Pearson, The Dief and Trudeau Oh my
Turner and Clark and . . .

Diox/Tox/Rob flash a giant puppet of the Prime Minister. Thundering noise. They yell 'Chin Muldoon.'

MULDOON: Who dares disturb the great Chin Muldoon? I said. Who dares disturb the great Chin Muldoon?

NADILKA: My name is Nintendo, uhh Nadilka and I represent the Indians from James Bay . . .

MULDOON: Go away! You naughty nonsensical nonvoter.

Nadilka runs back to group. Karuna Enters.

KARUNA: Dr. Karuna Kate here. And I want you to know Mr. Muldoon that I did a survey on the levels of mercury in the blood and . . .

MULDOON: Be quiet you misguided bleeding heart malpractical quack!!

Karuna runs back to group. Greenway approaches.

GREENWAY: What makes you think you could be so mean to us you chin-wagging windbag . . . Yeah!

MULDOON: Shut up!! No, come here, yes you, come here right now! Hurry up, come on. I know you don't I. You're the great Chief Greenway. I thought your hair would be straighter . . .

GREENWAY: I just got it done.
MULDOON: . . . and you'd be redder in the face.
GREENWAY: I didn't get much sun.
MULDOON: You're not half as bad as the newpapers claim you'd be.
GREENWAY: But I'm a real mean guy.
NADILKA: Please Mr Muldoon . . .
MULDOON: Speak when you are spoken too. After all this is a Democratic country.
GREENWAY: It's about the land.
MULDOON: Land? You got land?
GREENWAY: We used to . . .
MULDOON: How much do you want for it? Haven't got enough, wanna go condo. Wanna sign a land treaty? Come on speak up, what do you want?
GREENWAY: It's what they are doing to the land, it's that Megawatt project.
MULDOON: Resources, that's under Provincial jurisdiction. Now out of here, I'm a very busy man, the great Chin Muldoon is very busy. I've got fish to catch, a bush to hide behind . . . I

Nadilka, cued by the gong player discovers the actual voice behind the Chin.

Pay no attention to the man behind the statue of premier Bonaparte. He's a front man. A placebo, a janitor, a pooper-scooper ah ah ah . . . Hi.
DIOX/TOX/ROB: Hiiii.
NADILKA: You're the prime minister?
KARUNA: The great Chin Muldoon?
MULDOON: Ya but without the chin.
GREENWAY: It seems you can't do anything for us at all, can you?
MULDOON: Well no, see I really have no idea what I'm doing here at all. But when I talked to them they said that was the ideal job requirement.

Scene shifts to Thomas and Lubna. Diox/Tox/Rob exit top stage and re-enter main stage.

LUBNA: Now listen carefully. . . . We have to go away.

THOMAS: You are ready to leave the reserve? This must be my lucky day.

LUBNA: For intensive treatment.

THOMAS: What's that?

LUBNA: Well, the doctor found mercury in my blood. . . . She suspects the baby might be affected too.

THOMAS: My baby . . . Shit . . . This is great. It's the first time I'm going to be a father and my baby may be affected too. God . . . that's . . .

LUBNA: That's what Megawatt gave you.

THOMAS: But I worked for us. . . . For the baby too.

LUBNA: That's the price you pay.

THOMAS: You're trying to make me feel guilty? That is not fair. You had a hand in this too. You were told not to eat the fish. Why did you eat fish? Why didn't you stop eating fish?

Thomas shakes Lubna madly.

LUBNA: Thomas . . Stop!!

THOMAS: I don't want a deformed child.

LUBNA: Nobody wants a deformed child. That's the fear we got to live with.

THOMAS: I don't want to live in fear.

Scene shifts to Bonaparte's office. Diox/Tox/Rob parrot 'good' and do corresponding hand gestures.

BONAPARTE: Well, Brian did his usual puppet show, I presume. Even though I am the Premier, I cannot dictate affairs as they deem fit for the common good. There's an administrative board made up of individuals like these gentlemen, that should be responsible for deciding what's good for the common good. And that's good. In accordance with good political practice, I should hand over this report to this body, which shall be looked into by them and at a later date, decide what action to take, provided you do not go public, rocking the boat until the decision has been made. If by any chance, your concerns aren't addressed, they surely would be looked into after/during the second phase of Megawatt—Megawatt 2.

All clamour, cacophony.

OTHERS: Megawatt 2
KARUNA: Megawatt 2 . . . ? While children are dying of one?
DIOX/TOX/ROB: Children are replaceable.
KARUNA: So are you.

Diox/Tox/Rob scamper back to Bonaparte, crying like little children. We are living on the verge of a major catastrophe. You are blind, if you think I'll leave my report and go home. I'll release it independently to the press.

ROBERTTA: Can I talk to you alone doctor?
NATIVES: No!

Karuna agrees. The Diox/Tox/Rob mouths all the words in their speech regardless of who is actually talking.

ROBERTTA: My dear little lady
DIOX: I would expect that being a doctor.
TOX: You'd respect a basic fact
DIOX : That reports such as yours
TOX : Carry great potential
DIOX/TOX/ROB: For rumours
DIOX: And that's not fair to Megawatt 2.
TOX: Therefore, you must not do anything
ROBERTTA: That's not in conformity
DIOX: To the common interest of
DIOX/TOX/ROB: Jobs and progress.
KARUNA: Let the common people decide what's in the common interest.
TOX: I'm afraid
DIOX: He's afraid.
ROBERTTA: You have no choice . . .
DIOX: As an employee,

DIOX/TOX/ROB: Subordinate to Megawatt,
TOX: You have no right
ROBERTTA: To publicly express any opinion
DIOX: Which conflicts with the overall interest.
BONAPARTE: So I give you a choice to resign.
DIOX/TOX/ROB: Resign!
KARUNA: You're out of your mind.
ROBERTTA: I wanted you to say that, because now I can tell you. . . You're fired.

Diox/Tox/Rob mimes punching Karuna during the superlatives.

DIOX: Liquidated.
TOX: Jettisoned.
BONAPARTE: Sacked.
ROBERTTA: Dismissed.
DIOX: Terminated.
TOX: On your ass.
BONAPARTE: No longer needed.
ROBERTTA: On permanent vacation.
ALL: You're fired.
KARUNA: You have made my work much easier. As a doctor, I was trained to treat people in hospitals. As a citizen I'll cure a larger ill.

Karuna rushes off stage.

TOX: She is a dangerous woman
DIOX: Who doesn't use her heart but her head.
BONAPARTE: Keep an eye on her boys.
ROBERTTA: Don't worry, throwing stones at the government cannot harm those fellows up there stay intact.

Scene shifts to a newsvendor. Crowd surrounds vendor. Garbage bags are handed to each actor.

VENDOR: Extry, extry, extry . . . read all about it. New term for ecological sabotage—ecotage. . . . Anti pollution zorro terrorizes polluters.

CHORUS : Let me see the paper.

VENDOR: It costs a dollar. Extry, extry, extry . . . read all about it. Despite barricades, Megawatt still hires hundreds of Natives. Anti-pollution zorro putting up signs. . . . Look . . .

CHORUS: Where?!

Vendor points to Thomas and Lubna. All turn grasping their garbage bags.

THOMAS: All my life, I've worked to leave behind the fear—the fear of despair—the fear of my ancestors' past—the fear of uncertainty. And now when I'm to be a father, I have to live in fear of the uncertainty of my own child. No! I can't. You could have . . .

CHORUS : (*Whispering*) Ask her! Ask her!

THOMAS: . . . an abortion.

LUBNA: Are you crazy?

THOMAS: Abort.

LUBNA: Shut up.

THOMAS: I know it's hard, but I want a fear free complete child. How can we have a child when we know that the child may be disabled or poisoned?

LUBNA: So I can tell him it's his father's Megawatt that gave him the disability even before his birth.

THOMAS: And he will grow up hating me for all his life.

LUBNA: And remind you that you didn't do anything to fight against the source of his disability.

THOMAS: Let's be rational Lubna, you can have the abortion. We can go somewhere far far away.

LUBNA: Who are you? Who are you? There are more of our people in graves than there are alive. Not many of our people are left. Our children must live . . .

THOMAS: Why are you doing this to me?

LUBNA: You did this to me.

THOMAS: Shit!

LUBNA: It's fight that you never did for us. You never did it before. You'll never do it now. Just leave me . . .

THOMAS: Please Lubna . . . don't leave me.

Lubna runs into crowd. Crowd turns away from Thomas.

Lubna, come back!

SONG: Lubnaaaaaa, Lubnaaaaaaa,
Your pond your stream.
Your deer your dream.
Your forest your land.
Your friend your band.
Lubnaaaaaa, Lubnaaaaaaa,
Your corn your tree.
Your fish and sea.
Weed and root.
Flowers and shoot.
Lubnaaaaaa, Lubnaaaaaaa,

Come back, come back, come back, come back,
come back, come back, come back, come back.
Lubnaaaaaa.

Chorus freezes. One steps out facing the audience.

CHORUS: Ladies and gentlemen. This is Earth day brought to you by Dow Chemicals.

Picks up garbage bag and empties bag on tree, Lubna, Earth. All actors follow suit.

CHORUS: Alcan, Exxon, Inco, Hydro-Quebec. (*Cast repeats first chorus of song*)

All exit except Tree, Lubna, Earth.

EARTH: Lubna . . . Lubna . . . I'm the Earth.

LUBNA: I know, I am not performing my most sacred duty. I don't feed my child a mother's milk. I feed him mercury. It's in my blood . . . my milk.

TREE: Lubna . . . a mother who will breast feed pollution . . .

EARTH: I am dying too.
LUBNA: I've become an environmental refugee.

Chorus repeats each of Earth's words in a whisper

EARTH: Nightmares . . . air . . . pollution . . . breathe . . . poison . . . drink . . .
LUBNA: My child is dead. . . . No hope . . .
EARTH: Hopes live while people die. Why not live when you're alive.
Earth exits.

LUBNA: Can you find the burial ground?

Karuna enters.

KARUNA: Lubna . . .Who are you talking to?
LUBNA: I was talking to the earth. Where'd she go?
KARUNA: But . . . it can't be for real. . . . Was it a dream you were talking to the earth?
LUBNA: Didn't you see her?
KARUNA: I see it . . . yes, it's real . . .
LUBNA: You may not hear but she talks. And we talk back. Your people don't talk to us but the earth does.
KARUNA: Maybe I can drive you home. You look tired.
LUBNA: I'm going to the burial ground. My child is dead.
KARUNA: Sorry.
LUBNA: Don't bother. We got used to this a long time ago.

Lubna kisses Karuna and exits emotionless. She passes Thomas.

THOMAS: Lubna, I got laid off.

Karuna exits. Scene shifts to reporter.

TALKALOT: This is Mitsoumi Talkalot and I'm standing in front of Megawatt headquarters on Parizeau Blvd which houses the premier's office. An armed group of native Indians headed by Chief

Greenway have barricaded themselves inside the building since 3:23 pm yesterday afternoon. Their demands are yet unclear at the moment. Their actions seem to grow out of concerns about Megawatt phase 2 and it's environmental impact. The Premier has been quoted as saying "It seems they're pissed about some fish and might blow up the building." Pictures at 11. This is Mitsoumi Talkalot, Megawatt headquarters, Channel 101 News, Kwebec. And cut. How'd ya like that one? Not a bad accent eh?

Karuna approaches the barricade.

KARUNA: Chief Greenway.
GREENWAY: What do you want?
KARUNA: What are you doing here ?
GREENWAY: I've been talking to the trees.
KARUNA: I met Lubna. Her child is dead and she was talking to the earth.
GREENWAY: And did you believe her.
KARUNA: I want to do something. Let me in. I want to talk to you. I have to join you. We have to win them over. But you can't do it this way.
GREENWAY: You are mistaken doctor. We have to act.
KARUNA: But they're listening to the Indians now.
GREEENWAY: Words . . . But nothing has changed. 400 years ago thousands of our people died due to diseases transmitted to them by invaders. They should have built a blockade on our country then.
KARUNA: Well, you can't wage a war in 1990.
GREENWAY: Why not? We have tried everything else. A bunch of Indians walk on foot for 500 miles or sail across the border to draw attention to our plight, showing their ancient transport skills and we end up as a tourist attraction for the passersby. A handful of white environmentalists greet us while New Kids on the Block make the headline news.
KARUNA: That's the problem. You want to win America back for Indian people and do it through warrior society and barricades. You won't be heard unless Canadian people are with you.
GREENWAY: Canadian people?

KARUNA: Yes, Canadian people. The white people as you call them. We have a role in the matter, too. That is why I am here. If you go to the extremes, the government has a perfect case against you. If you take the law into your own hands, people don't like it. Do you know what your Minister of Indian Affairs calls you? "Armed Bandits."

GREENWAY: I don't remember choosing a Minister for our affairs.

KARUNA: I know. But people like law and order. They don't like thugs. When you set up barricades, you look like thugs. Why are you hiding your faces?

Karuna starts pulling down their hankercheifs only to find . . . Nadilka.

KARUNA: This violence won't do any good.

GREENWAY: Violence . . .Who is talking about violence?

KARUNA: Blowing up this building?

GREENWAY: Doctor, we haven't any dynamite.

KARUNA: Every news report says you do.

GREENWAY: What do you mean, who told you that, it's a lie. Tell them, it's all a lie. We have no dynamite.

KARUNA: If you give them the slightest chance, they'll put you in jail. And you can't do anything behind bars. That's what they want. Don't give them the chance. The environmental movement has done one good thing. It has brought the plight of the native people to the headlines. Many people right now sympathize with you. Take advantage of that.

GREENWAY: Let her in.

Karuna walks through barricade. Scene shifts to premiers Diox/Tox/Rob.

ROBERTTA: We have to get back to James Bay and tell the media what a great idea Megawatt is. We have to tell our side of the story.

Scene shifts to barricade.

GREENWAY: You are not one of us unless you have something of us.

KARUNA: What do you mean?

GREENWAY: White man has never gone from here empty handed.

KARUNA: White woman.

GREENWAY: My grandmother gave me this necklace. I want you to have it.

KARUNA: But . . . It's from your grandmother.

GREENWAY: She gave me this when she was dying . . . and said "Our people are not left in great numbers, Care for them." I give you this with the same sentiment.

KARUNA: Thank you.

Scene shifts to reporter.

TALKALOT: This is Mitsumi Talkalot coming to you from Channel 101 News. The Premier has just arrived.

Bonaparte enters with Diox/Tox/Rob and stands in front of media.

TOX: Hello Canada. May I have your attention please. Thank you. It's our pleasure to invite the man who oversaw the Megawatt project along with subsidiary industries, to invite the far sighted premier Bob Bonaparte, the mastermind behind Megawatt Project.

Bonaparte moves forward.

BONAPARTE: Ladies and gentlemen and my distinguished friends from the reserve, I take pride in pursuing the great vision of my great ancestors of taming the river, reshaping the land and using the forest for a common interest of greater good. Megawatt 2 is a success story of Megawatt 1 and I am proud to be associated with this project. It seems you Indians have a little trouble. (*Looks to Diox/Tox/Rob*) What's the problem.

TOX: The fish.

DIOX: Swimming caribou.

ROBERTTA: Mini-putt or something.

BONAPARTE: Oh yeah! Come on. We can talk about this. My office is always open, but you should know, . . . you're in it. Look, he's got his feet on my desk. . . . We're always willing to listen to you people. Hell, we've been listening to your problems for over 400 years now. Let me in. We'll let all these nice media people go home.

REPORTER: With all the negotiations going on, what exactly does Prime Minister Muldoon have to play?

BONAPARTE: Mary, that is a very good question. In fact, that question is the best question I've heard this week. That question, Mary . . . Mumbles I'd like to ask him that myself.

TELEGRAM: Telegram for Mr. Bonaparte, from Prime Minister Muldoon. Dear Bob. Stop. How're you doing? Question Mark. Stop. With all your talk of Sovereignty. Stop. I wanted to see how you do on your own. Stop. How's it going, Bob? Question mark. Stop. Love Chin. Stop. P.S. My Irish eyes are smiling. Stop. End. That'll be $17.99 with the G.S.T.

BONAPARTE: Get outta here!

TELEGRAM: (*Aside*) Cheapskate.

GREENWAY: You can't go ahead with another Megawatt phase without genuine public inquiry.

BONAPARTE: There has been . . .

DIOX/TOX/ROB: (*To Bob*) No, not really sir.

GREENWAY: Not the one where you are judge and your buddies are the jury.

BONAPARTE: I object to this statement.

DIOX/TOX/ROB: We resemble that remark.

KARUNA: We won't let you go Mr. Bonaparte without listening to our statement publicly.

BONAPARTE: What kind of talk is that? In front of all these nice people? What kind of talk is that? You can't take me hostage.

KARUNA: You aren't a hostage Mr. Bonaparte. You are a public leader in a public place, watched by the national public on public T.V. And we wish to make a public statement.

BONAPARTE: No way! If you want to talk, come to my office.

GREENWAY: It's talks you do endlessly but we are tired of talk. We want you to listen now. Friends, Megawatt must go through scrutiny to determine its environmental and cultural devastation before phase 2 gets going. The environmental impact assessment has been fabricated and tampered with. We demand proper legislation be put into effect so that no industry could ram through environmentally unsafe projects due to lack of legislation. When there can be a full scale hearing on a jogging path on Mount Royal, why not Megawatt for proposed flooding and construction of power line and roads? We will surrender this building when the government puts down its whistle-in-the-dark strategy for we owe to our children fresh air, unpoisoned water and the right to live on the land. (*To Bonaparte*) Now that we have appealed to the people, you are welcome to do the same. But we will not allow anything without a review.

BONAPARTE: The matter will be taken care of . . . yeah. Time out . . . ten minute recess. (*To Diox/Tox/Rob*) This is appalling. I'm dying to deliver my self written speech and somebody steals the show. These people are winning the hearts of all Canadians. Even the army is undecided. Time for a scandal.

ROBERTTA: Something has to be done.

ALL: Once and for all.

TOX: Let's blow up the building and blame it on the Indians.

DIOX: Yeah. I already told the media. They had tonnes of dynamite.

BONAPARTE: Way to go!

TOX: Where do we get that much dynamite?

All look to Robertta.

ROBERTTA: Knowing the situation probably wouldn't just blow over, remember that little dynamite heist out in St. Kaboom, well, they got the wrong guys, it's in my rec room.

BONAPARTE: But if we blow up the building, we'll cripple our hydro network.

ROBERTTA: What's another blackout.

TOX: Remember solar flares.

BONAPARTE: But of course, with the blackout the Indians will have insurmountable PR problems. Oh, goody. I always wanted to blame someone else for my blackouts.

TOX: Give the moose a break.

ROBERTTA: What's the plan?

They huddle and shuffle off stage. Press follows asking questions. Gang repeats, "no comment." Diox/Tox/Rob slinks across stage with dynamite. They arrive at barricade with dynamite hidden. There is knock on the door.

ROBERTTA: Dr. Karuna Cate.
KARUNA: Yes.
ROBERTTA: We would like to talk to you.
KARUNA: Yes.
ROBERTTA: We would like to see if you would be prepared to be on the assessment board that you suggested on national T.V.
KARUNA: What about him?
ROBERTTA: Oh yeah, Chief Greenway too. Just let us in and we'll talk about it.
GREENWAY: Sure, let them in.

Chorus teaches Bonaparte how to wire detonator.

KARUNA: What do you want to talk about?
ROBERTTA: Hey, nice barricade.
TOX: Yeah, didn't I see this in Better Roads and Blockades.
DIOX: Yeah, April issue. My, I'm feeling a little peckish. How about you? (*To Tox*)
TOX: No. We just ate. (*Diox nudges him*) Oh, yeah. Starved. How about pizza?
ROBERTTA: Any of those big strong handsome warrior types around with those cute little bazookas or are there just us five?
GREENWAY: No, just the doctor and I.
ROBERTTA: That's pizza for five.
GREENWAY: Duck!

They fight. Diox/Tox/Rob tie up doctor and chief. Robertta takes necklace off doctor's neck and throws it on ground. Meanwhile Diox and Tox plant the dynamite. Explosion. Whole cast falls to floor.

TALKALOT: This is Mitsumi Talkalot standing in front of the blazing inferno that once was Megawatt Headquarters. Thousands of homes and businesses have been crippled by this major explosion. It seems the natives have carried out their threats because their demands have not been met. Two people known to be in the building at the time are still unaccounted for. They are the leaders of the native movement. Dr. Karuna Cate and Chief Scott Greenwag. We are lucky to have with us right now a representative from the Premier's office . . . oops, former office. Miss Robertta Notaway. She was in the building with the two leaders fifteen minutes before the explosion. (*Turns to Robertta*) You were the last living person known to have talked to the people . . .

ROBERTTA: I can't believe this has happened. We were in there discussing the preparation of the assessment board for Megawatt 2. There was so much tension in the room. Chief Greenway kept repeating that if his demands weren't met, he would blow up the building and create blackouts throughout Kwebec, crippling the entire province. Tempers were flaring and the heat was on. It was a powderkeg of emotions, but I just want to say. You've been crying shame, shame, shame on us. They say there's dark pools of misery and injustice; that they exist in this country. We can't go back in time and reverse everything. They say that we have cultural deserts, racial discrimination; that this was the Indian's land first. It's true, it's all true. But where's the pride? The pride because we do try to attack these flaws. We do make headway. Our goals are high and we achieve so much. But where's the balance that says "we're only human," and the human condition is not perfect. Give thanks that we have high standards and, being human, we have done as much as we have. We have a damned fine country. Yes, it's in trouble, but show me a better one.

Lights fade to darkness. Pause.

GREENWAY: Hey turn those lights back on. 'Dark pools of misery'? 'We're only human' 'Where's the pride'? What a happy ending. Patriotic crap!! It makes me want to throw up. Where's the justice here?! How about a happy ending for us.

Repeat of explosion.

TALKALOT: This is Mitsumi Talkalot still standing in front of the blazing inferno that once was Megawatt Headquarters. Thousands of homes and businesses have been crippled by this major explosion. It was first assumed that the natives were responsible for this catastrophe. It has now come to our attention that the Premier and his aides are being held by the Surete on a charge of conspiracy to destroy public property. It seems we now have reports of an eye 'witness who saw the Premier and his aides unloading dynamite from the back of a hydro quebec truck into Megawatt headquarters.

ROBERTTA: An eyewitness!

TOX: Someone saw us?

DIOX: Me too!

TALKALOT: We now have an exclusive interview with the boy and his dog.

A blindman enters, looking for the camera.

KARUNA: My necklace, my necklace.

Earth holds Dr. Karuna's head in her hands. Tree moves closer. Natives form semicircle around necklace. Lubna moves forward to pick up necklace.

CAST MEMBER: One time, I wished myself into a moose deer.
I was lying down, sleeping in my shadow.
And then you came along.
Saying the sun was in your mouth.
Saying you were thirsty .
I wished you to where you drank tears.
It was a lake everyone cried into.
Full of people's tears.
At night
Some of the tears left
To look for sad faces to fall down.
Then the whole lake cried.
Some, they said it was the loons.

Lubna, with determination, places necklace on tree.

TRADING INJURIES

The backdrop of this story is 1948 partition of India into India and Pakistan whereby Pakistan was created as a "new country" exclusively for the muslims. But like most muslims Jeena's parents decided to stay back in India for it was their country. She was only five at the time of partition. But the life was never the same for muslims in India after its division. Communal violence erupted year after year between India's muslim minority and segments of fanatics from among the hindu majority.

22 years after the partition, Jeena and her husband Qaiser Quraishi flee from India with their one year old daughter to save their lives as their ancestral home is destroyed in a communal riot. They land in Montreal, Canada as refugees.

Qaiser has brought a charred brick with him from his old ancestral home to remind himself what he had in his old country. The brick serves as an inspiration for him to buy a new home in his new country. Starting as a factory worker he works his way up to the manager's post. Some years later he becomes co-owner of "Teja's Tandoori Dhaba"—a rundown restaurant run by his sikh friend Teja Singh. Jeena on the other hand puts aside her dream of becoming a school teacher for she must support her husband's quest to buy a brick-house and bring up their daughter. She works in a sweat factory during the day and does piece work at home in her "spare" time.

After Quebec's first sovereignty referendum, the house prices hit bottom low and Quraishis buy their first home in Canada. But now all their earnings go to pay off the mortgage. And the work continues to take toll on Jeena's health. Her veins are popping out from under the skin of her legs and her lungs are showing signs of irreversible injury, probably due to her work in the sweat factory. According to Dr. Khaber, if she doesn't stop working, her injuries will cripple her completely. In the mean time, with the resurgence of the separatist movement in Quebec, Qaiser's factory shuts down.

Now the family has to come up with a way to pay off the mortgage in order to save their home or move out. Dr. Khaber advises Jeena to sue the factory for compensation and save the family home from being taken over by the bank. Jeena deals with the dilemma—"trading injuries is the price she has to pay in order to save her house"?

"Trading Injuries" explores the human cost of people once already dispossessed of their country and of their homes.

CHARACTERS

QAISER QURAISHI:	An immigrant from India
JEENA QURAISHI:	Qaiser's wife
TEJA SINGH:	A Sikh, friend of Qaiser
SAMREEN:	Qaiser and Jeena's daughter. She comes in the play as five year old, 10 year old and a twenty year old woman
MARTIN:	Factory worker
MARIE-FRANCE:	Waitress at Teja's Tandoori Dhaba
BERNIE:	Cloth merchant
DR. KHABER:	Jeena's doctor

Reviews

The play produces some strong and searing images of immigrant life in our supposedly democratic country.

Montreal Downtowner

("Trading Injuries") contains piercing observations and witty lines, . . . It's got heart, guts and an original point of view.

The Gazette

Late 1979-80 Montreal, a major city of the province of Quebec. Separatist campaign to take Quebec out of Canada is in the air.

The set consists of a big family room with large windows and two doors leading to other rooms, a hallway and a staircase suggesting the second floor. Behind it, at an angle from the house, one can see the front of a restaurant. A small medical clinic is also situated on one side. Behind the restaurant and the medical clinic, there is a suggesstion of a factory in the background. There is an old deserted apartment, which is situated way back, in a metaphorical sense.

As the play opens, we hear sounds of arriving car and incoming voices of Jeena, Qaiser, Samreen (10 years old), and Teja who have just walked up the outside of the house to inspect it.

QAISER: Look at this house. Two storeys, balcony, a lawn and a backyard, two car garages and a church within two blocks. . . . But still the price did not hit the sky. Thank you God.

TEJA: Don't thank God. Thank Mr. Levesque and his sovereignty referendum.

QAISER: It is a bargain.

SAMREEN: Baba, whose house was this?

QAISER: It is going to be ours.

SAMREEN: I mean whose house was it before.

QAISER: I don't know. Jeena how do you like it?

JEENA: Good.

QAISER: That's it—just good?

JEENA: It is good.

QAISER: What is on your mind Jeena?

JEENA: Has the previous owner left Quebec?

QAISER: That is not my concern. All that matters to me is that this is what I want. It is buyer's market out there Jeena. If I don't buy now, I never will.

TEJA: So is the passion politics.

Flashback sounds in Jeena's mind—mob violence, gun fire, people running, children crying etc. These sounds gradually increase throughout the next few lines.

JEENA: Thank you passion politics? It is the passion that drove us out of our home 10 years ago . . . and half of our family before

that from their ancestral home.
TEJA: You mean partition of India.
JEENA: I was only a child and I still have nightmares of that . . .

Sound of chaos grows louder

TEJA: But nobody is forced to leave Quebec.

Sound comes to an end.

JEENA: Yeah, they are made to leave.
TEJA: No, they are made to vote. Remember the referendum?
JEENA: Wonderful. Civilization at last.
QAISER: Jeena I did not come here to hear about the misfortunes of those who had to leave their homes. I came to show you the house that I want to buy because now is the time to buy our own house. We need this house because we don't have anything here. Nobody to protect us and nobody to guide us. We need this house for Samreen. Okay.
TEJA: Like other immigrants—invest in a house not in the stock market, so that the immigrant children can inherit a secure future.
SAMREEN: I haven't even seen it from inside.
QAISER: Let's go inside.

Lights brighten on the interior of the house. Everybody walks in.

QAISER: Look at these large windows, the high ceiling, look at the marble floor, look at the fireplace.
SAMREEN: (*Looking out of the window*) Look at the church right from the window. I can hear the church bells right from the bed room.

She runs out through the doors and comes running back.

And wow — two bathrooms!
TEJA: Can't afford to be constipated in this house.
SAMREEN: Baba, I am impressed.
QAISER: You know what? I am going to give you the best room.

SAMREEN: Why me?

QAISER: Because in our old sub-basement apartment, your mother told me every day that Samreen should have the best room.

SAMREEN: Thanks ma.

JEENA: I said every girl should have her own room in the house while growing to be an adult.

SAMREEN: And soon I am going to be a complete adult with complete adult features.

QAISER: Tut, tut. Think before you open your mouth. Just because you are more Canadian than we are is no reason to act like them.

SAMREEN: O.K. I love the house and I would love to have my own room.

QAISER: But remember . . . no friends in dirty sneakers.

SAMREEN: What do you mean? I can't have my friends over?

QAISER: You won't be allowed to mess up the house, especially my Indian carpets.

SAMREEN: That's no fun.

QAISER: We are going to keep it sparkling clean. We are going to show the world we are here and we are here to stay for all our life. Teja my friend, you met us the first day we came to Canada. And you are with us today when I am buying my first house.

TEJA: Typical immigrant. Remember everything they do first in the new country.

QAISER: That is right mister. I remember and I want to thank you very much for every thing.

Flashback: sound of arriving ship is heard as the lights begin to change and we go in flashback. Street sounds of Canada in the seventies. Winter setting in. Jeena and Qaiser, younger but tired, are standing on the street with a broken suitcase and another bundle of luggage. Jeena is holding a baby (Samreen) in her arms. Looking lost, they unsuccessfully try to cross the street amid sound of fast passing cars. Teja appears on the other side of the street and observes the couple curiously. Qaiser and Jeena notice him.

QAISER: Hey mister.

TEJA: Calling me?

QAISER: Yes sir.

TEJA: Just got off the boat?

QAISER: Yes please.

TEJA: First time in Canada?

QAISER: Yes.

TEJA: It shows. Canada is mighty cold 8 months of the year. Wrap your baby in something warmer before the baby catches pneumonia.

QAISER: Yes sir.

TEJA: Don't wait for the snowfall. The national sport here is ice hockey, you know, not field hockey. Come on, let's get you out of the cold before the baby freezes completely. Just around the corner is YMCA, the shelter for international arrivals. We can sit and talk there.

They cross the street and arrive in the YMCA cafeteria which is represented by a table and few chairs.

TEJA: By the way, my name is Teja Singh.

QAISER: I am Qaiser Quraishi. This is my wife Jeena and this is our baby Samreen.

TEJA: What a peaceful little baby. Never cries.

The baby cries.

Oh, you little cheater. Any trouble at the immigration?

QAISER: They accepted our refugee status.

TEJA: The government won't let you die once you are here. But it is worried. Too many refugees.

QAISER: From where?

TEJA: Mainly from ex-colonies. Some are running from persecution, others "plan" on becoming refugees.

JEENA: Nobody plans on becoming a refugee.

TEJA: Oh, the bogus ones do. And they are avid planners. Plan everything, right down to their proof of persecution—an instant snapshot taken in front of a burnt-out shop. Now they spend their days waiting for their refugee hearings. Thank you Canadian tax payers.

JEENA: We did not want to be refugees.

TEJA: Do you know I am a sikh from the Pakistan side of the border?

JEENA: You don't look sikh.

TEJA: Just because I am not wearing my turban? Well, with a turbanless head I don't look sikh. But I had to change my appearance just to escape alive. Ah, well, such were the times and such was the racial hatred. Now I am a weekend sikh. I put on the turban on the weekends only when I have to go for weekly worships. Hah. . . . Have to keep the culture alive you know. Rest of the time they take me for a Hindu who prays faithfully to 1000 different Gods. I'd rather not say anything about the muslims—minimum punishment death.

JEENA: I wouldn't dare say a word about any one of them.

TEJA: They hate each other just the same.

JEENA: Here, too?

TEJA: Here too.

QAISER: In Canada?

TEJA: In Canada.

JEENA: Oh dear God.

TEJA: (*Laughing*) God does it to them. Can you imagine a Hindu praying 5 times a day like a true muslim? Or a muslim worshipping a phallic symbol like a true hindu? Or either one of them with a 7 yard long turban and a dagger around the shoulder like a true sikh. Funny!—immigrants become more religious once they come to Canada.

JEENA: So they fight with each other here, too.

TEJA: Oh, no. Sometimes they take a break—like when they decide to fight against racism in the Canadian system.

JEENA: Excuse me!

TEJA: Canada will teach you some of life's hard realities. Everybody makes it in the end, though. Now what you need most is a roof over your head, a kitchen to cook and a sitting room to watch TV like all other immigrants.

QAISER: That sounds like a good idea.

TEJA: I'll fix things up with the landlord. Nice pot bellied man. Cheap but not too cheap. I will help you buy few household things from the co-op.

JEENA: Co-op?

TEJA: Co-operation!

JEENA: Co-operation?

TEJA: Leftist minded white folks run it for needy families.

JEENA: Salvation army?

TEJA: Something like that. After all your countrymen don't believe in co-ops. Na na. First thing they set up is a mosque . . . or temple or a gurdwara.

JEENA: Please.

TEJA: They get an emergency fund set up to import a preacher from India.

JEENA: Didn't we have enough of them already ?

TEJA: (*Sarcastically*) They serve your religious needs.

JEENA: I need pots and pans, Teja.

TEJA: Sorry, God doesn't care much for practical needs.

QAISER: We are lucky we met you. I don't know what we would have done without you.

TEJA: The pleasure is all mine. (*Laughs*)

His laughter blends with the music as the lights come back to the house. Flashback ends.

JEENA: So will you stand and thank each other or do whatever you have to do next.

QAISER: We thank the real real estate genius and we move in.

Music begins. Teja and Qaiser shake hands, hug etc. Samreen runs inside as Jeena starts to work and set up the house, giving it a life. Surprisingly, she puts up a brick on a shelf which remains prominently visible throughout the play. As she works, we hear Jeena's internal voice.

Note: Throughout the play, Jeena's internal voice can be played out on a tape or she can deliver it herself, depending on Director's choice.

JEENA: (*Internal*) . . . . Moved in we did into this beautiful duplex. It took us eleven years of hard labour and careful supervision of poverty. And I worked like a dog. Part-time, full time, overtime all the time. Because Qaiser wanted to buy a house. No matter what sacrifices I had to make and no matter what I had to do. I knew it will be hard in the beginning but did I know the beginning will last for ever? And Qaiser, who has been fixated on buying this house, would like me to believe that the things will be different for me now!!! Huh.

Jeena curiously looks at the brick as Qaiser arrives.

QAISER: Don't you miss not having that horrible, smelly, sordid rotting sub-basement apartment we lived for 10 years.

JEENA: I do. Because I am so used to clean, scrape, wax and polish. I think I have decorated this house beautifully.

QAISER: That's for sure.

JEENA: Superb dress maker, superb factory worker and superb house maker.

QAISER: Do I detect sarcasm?

JEENA: When do the facts become sarcasm?

Qaiser walks over to the brick.

QAISER: Jeena, I wasn't a fool to have brought a charred brick all the way from India.

JEENA: I know that Qaiser.

QAISER: This brick is all the memory I have of my home back home.

JEENA: (*Pointing at the shelf*) The memory is well preserved in the middle shelf of the cabinet.

QAISER: The upstairs tenant has decided to stay on. We can renegotiate the rent once his previous lease expires. But I feel uncomfortable talking to him about money.

JEENA: Then don't talk about money.

QAISER: There is so much I want to talk to you and not about money. There is so much we have been missing. . . .

JEENA: Have we been missing something?

QAISER: For too long. Jeena we have a great bedroom and before we forget all about it . . . especially when our teenage daughter is not home.

Qaiser locks her in his arms.

JEENA: What is it with you Qaiser?
QAISER: Remember, how we used to meet before we got married.
JEENA: I remember.
QAISER: You used to hang a green towel on your window to let me know that no one was home. And I used to sneak into your house.

JEENA: I was young then.
QAISER: Let me care for you the way I used to. Please . . . come.

He kisses her.

JEENA: Stop.
QAISER: Jeena I am your husband.
JEENA: And so you think you can ask me anything.
QAISER: I sure can. Take this saree off.
JEENA: Qaiser we are growing old for that sort of thing.
QAISER: That is why we should not wait any longer.
JEENA: It is funny the way you display your middle age hormonal imbalance.
QAISER: How long is this saree? God, Indian women wear too many clothes.
JEENA: And western women wear too little.
QAISER: And waste little time.
JEENA: I envy them.
QAISER: Why? Why after so many years in Canada, you still wear a saree. . . . Eh . . . Help me unwind it.
JEENA: NO!!!
QAISER: What's wrong? Feeling shy with me?
JEENA: I don't want you to see my body. Even I am frightened to see it. It is not the same any more.
QAISER: Doesn't matter to me.
JEENA: You don't understand.
QAISER: What?
JEENA: The ugly flab of flesh which waddles around my waist. Veins which are popping out from under the skin of my legs. Look like the map of the world. That's what I cover under the six

yard long saree.

QAISER: I can switch off the lights.

JEENA: You don't get it, do you? I can't do it.

QAISER: I was just seeking some affection.

JEENA: You can't understand that.

Qaiser leaves the room. Lights narrow on Jeena. She sits facing the audiences as we hear her internal voice.

JEENA: (*Internal*) . . . . How long have I gone on denying that this was coming. How long have I tried to convince myself that this condition is normal because all the women in the factory have swollen legs. God—the more I deny, more I hate myself and more I hate myself, more I deny. And I don't know why? What will I tell the doctor? That I missed the bus by 10 steps because I couldn't walk fast enough. That I was busy setting up the new house? Why have I waited that long to visit my doctor? Fear? Maybe I know what she is going to tell me. She will tell me to stop working. I wish it was as easy for me to do as it has been for her to say that.

Lights fade out on Jeena. Fade in on the medical clinic. Dr. Khaber is reading a report. Jeena walks over to the clinic.

KHABER: I have here your test results Jeena. And I have some questions.

JEENA: I will try to answer Dr. Khaber.

KHABER: Does anybody else in the family have a history of such symptoms?

JEENA: You mean stiffening of the muscles ?

KHABER: And breathing discomfort.

JEENA: No.

KHABER: No tuberculosis?

JEENA: Not to my knowledge.

KHABER: Jeena, do you remember having this discomfort, before you started working in the sweat factory?

JEENA: I don't remember seeing so much smoke and such noisy machines in my life.

KHABER: Has any health inspector ever visited your work place?

JEENA: Doctor, I went to the factory to work, not to get involved in politics.

KHABER: But somebody should care about what is going on.

JEENA: When something goes wrong, they will take care of it.

KHABER: Like?

JEENA: Like there is this man who comes every month.

KHABERWith a sandwich in one hand and coffee in another. And laughs (*Mocking*) har har har . . .

JEENA: After every line.

KHABER: That must be the union boss. But I am not worried about general grievances. My concern is your health. Did anybody in your factory ever make you fill out a health questionnaire? If yes, I would like to see it.

JEENA: I don't recall anything of that kind.

KHABER: Nobody from the government?

JEENA: No.

KHABER: Now you know whom to blame when someone dies in the sweat factory.

JEENA: What?

KHABER: I am terribly sorry. That was very unprofessional of me. I guess I am frustrated with the lack of action.

JEENA: But what about my treatment?

KHABER: Oh yes. I almost forgot. I am ordering some more tests. I will treat you for the medical side of it now and deal with the official side later.

JEENA: Official side?

KHABER: If this is a work related thing or a long term disability or anything else. In the mean time, as a precaution maybe you should consider quitting the factory.

JEENA: Doctor, I have to work.

KHABER: Jeena you have already bought your house.

JEENA: Now we have to pay off the mortgage. Besides, a second pay cheque is a big help.

KHABER: I mean there must be some other kind of work.

JEENA: I did a second job too. More sewing.

KHABER: Piece work at home?

JEENA: For this man called Bernie.

KHABER: Another low salary and no benefit job.

JEENA: Doctor, we bought a house. Not with the earnings but with the savings and overtime

KHABER: I can understand that. My folks are first generation immigrants too.

JEENA: Doctor, the work is what gives me my pride. Besides I have a daughter to send to university.

KHABER: I understand. As your doctor, it is good to know your background. Well here is your prescription and please make another appointment. I would like to visit your home some time. Is that alright?

JEENA: You are most welcome, any time.

KHABER: I'd like to meet your husband too.

JEENA: Then you have to call first. Sometimes he works at night.

KHABER: Where?

JEENA: Teja's Tandoori Dhaba. It is a restaurant. My husband is part owner.

Lights cross fade to the restaurant. The sign reads Teja's Tandoori Dhaba. An ear wrenching popular Indian film music is heard. Teja arrives at the front counter.

TEJA: Marie-France.

MARIE-FRANCE: In the kitchen.

TEJA: Factory is out.

MARIE-FRANCE: I hope they pay their bills.

TEJA: Stop serving them on credit. We need paying customers.

MARIE-FRANCE: I don't know what is it? Bad government or recession, or what?

TEJA: Call it re-surgence.

MARIE-FRANCE: What is that?

TEJA: Re-surgence of shipload of separatists, Captain Jacques Parizeau in control.

MARIE-FRANCE: Don't they remember the last referendum? The separatists lost their pants.

TEJA: You know there is a saying in India, "you can't straighten a dog's tail even if you bury it straight in the ground for eight years."

MARIE-FRANCE: All I want to straighten up is our customers. For goodness sake—We need money a whole lot more than the strip joints do.

TEJA: What do you know about strip joints.

MARIE-FRANCE: Where do you think I met Martin? I don't want to go back to cha-cha chaing buck naked for a bunch of toothless old men. Here comes Martin.

Enters Martin.

TEJA: Martin, we were just talking about you.

MARTIN: I don't care.

MARIE-FRANCE: You had a run in with somebody.

TEJA: I will leave you two love birds alone.

MARIE-FRANCE: So Martin!

MARTIN: I need official protection.

MARIE-FRANCE: Is someone after you?

MARTIN: My living standards are going down the toidy.

MARIE-FRANCE: What are you going to do to up them?

MARTIN: Send all the greaseballs back to where they came from.

MARIE-FRANCE: Martin shut up.

MARTIN: Rid the factory of them.

MARIE-FRANCE: Shhh. . . .

MARTIN: And the country.

MARIE-FRANCE: Did you leave your brain at the assembly line or what?

MARTIN: I know your problem.

MARIE-FRANCE: Enlighten me Martin.

MARTIN: You are colour-blind.

MARIE-FRANCE: Oh really!

MARTIN: Look around you, hordes of coloured women. One baby pulling her saree, another in her arm and one in her belly. Only fun they got is breeding year round. I think the government should do a survey.

MARIE-FRANCE: Survey?

MARTIN: Survey of their breeding habits. But instead what it gives them—baby bonus! Cash for kids. Do you bring any bonus home?

MARIE-FRANCE: I am not a breeding factory.

MARTIN: You are not patriotic. Give them 50 years and we will be the visible minority. Bunch of kids singing the Canadian anthem in Punjabi, with their twisted tongues.
MARIE-FRANCE: (*Clenching teeth*) You better watch your tongue.
MARTIN: And this manager guy at my factory—Qaiser.
MARIE-FRANCE: He is my boss too. Part owner of the Dhaba.
MARTIN: Bloody paki.
MARIE-FRANCE: You shut up Martin. Teja is not too far.
MARTIN: He is another paki.
MARIE-FRANCE: Shhh. He might hear you.
MARTIN: Doesn't he know?
MARIE-FRANCE: What's your problem Martin?
MARTIN: This dwarf Qaiser.
MARIE-FRANCE: What about him?
MARTIN: He ain't tall enough.
MARIE-FRANCE: Is that why you look down on him?
MARTIN: The guy had to climb on a three inch thick brick to reach the machine. He carried a Goddamn brick with him. And look where he is now. Before I could spit, he got a business, sucked up to a manager post and bought himself a house.
MARIE-FRANCE: Martin, he is coming. You better think before you open your mouth.
MARTIN: Hell that's just how I talk. I tell the way it is.

Enters Qaiser.

QAISER: Hello Marie-France. Martin. (*Pause*) What's the matter? No talk? Where is Teja?

Teja enters.

TEJA: Assalam-wale-kum Qaiser.
QAISER: Wale-kum-salam. So what will it be for you Martin? Rum or scotch or a double draft.
MARTIN: It's okay.
QAISER: Martin I know why you are upset. But I don't think you understand.
MARTIN: Oh yeah.

QAISER: Let me explain.

MARTIN: (*Outburst*) You let go three of my buddies. What are you going to do next? Stop me from taking my union break? Blackmail me by dangling more refugees in front of my face?

QAISER: Mr. Banks makes the decisions.

MARTIN: There are rules in this country. Have you heard of rules. R.U.L.E.S.

QAISER: Look Martin . . .

MARTIN: Don't order me. I am on my own time. I'll say what I fucking well please.

QAISER: I don't fire any body. Mr Banks orders me and . . .

MARTIN: You order us.

QAISER: I have to do my job.

MARTIN: What job? Hire more of your kind.

QAISER: Your kind don't do the shit jobs that my kind do. You know that.

MARTIN: Why should they? Why should they work for peanuts.

QAISER: You know what your problem is? You think you own this country.

MARTIN: Damn, How long have I been in this country?

TEJA: Martin, did you have a bad day?

MARIE FRANCE: I think he had a rough day.

MARTIN: My great grandfather was born here. My grandfather was born here, my father was born here, my mother was born here. I was born here. My dog was born here. But it's me who lives in the dog house.

MARIE-FRANCE: Every dog has his day.

TEJA: Martin, this man is your boss.

MARTIN: This man is a job stealer himself.

QAISER: Martin you are so stupid, you are so typically stupid, you can't even figure out that if it was so damn easy to steal, I would have stolen something better.

MARTIN: Oh yeah! How did you become a manager?

QAISER: I worked hard. If you have a bit of self respect work as hard as I do.

MARTIN: I would rather live on welfare than work for less than what I deserve.

MARIE-FRANCE: Martin go home.

MARTIN: Don't order me around. I will go when I please. (*Pause*) Bye.

MARIE-FRANCE: I am sorry Qaiser.

QAISER: It is not your fault.

MARIE-FRANCE: I can't believe this drivelling idiot is my boyfriend. Trust me, I will have a serious talk with him.

QAISER: Not on my account, because I am going to give him a chance to see how hard I worked.

TEJA: Marie-France, I think you can go home. I will lock up.

MARIE-FRANCE: Thanks. Bye.

QAISER: God I hate it.

TEJA: Just ignore it.

QAISER: How? No matter what, somebody will always make me feel guilty for anything and everything I do. Does he think I enjoyed lining up in front of the factory before sunrise in below twenty cold? Twenty years in this country and feels like I just landed in this country.

Flashback: Qaiser throws a glass which crashes against the wall. Sound blends into ship hooter leading us back to 1970 when his family had just arrived.

TEJA: Don't you worry Mr. and Mrs. Quraishi. They do things to the newcomers that they don't do to their own poor. And while we are at it, have you got any money?

JEENA: Only my gold jewellery. .

TEJA: Enough to invest? Like, say, 250,000 dollars.

JEENA: 250,000 dollars?

QAISER: Then you better look for a job. They will ask you "have you got any Canadian experience?"

QAISER: I don't.

TEJA: Then they will tell you "no Canadian experience, no job".

JEENA: How do you know?

TEJA: That's my Canadian experience.

JEENA: Then what are we going to do?

TEJA: Canada has got tons of factories for you. That's where Mr. Byron Banks comes in.

JEENA: Who?

TEJA: A man who knows a good bargain when he sees one. So I will take your husband down to the factory to meet Mr. Banks.

QAISER: Factory?

TEJA: That is right. You can kiss your degrees good bye. Mr. Banks believes in hard work not paper work. He would want you to use your hands not your brain. He would want you to be a family man who would not join union or go on strike. And he will pay you more than you could ever make in your country.

QAISER: But I am not in my country anymore.

TEJA: Then he will remind you about your work visa. There are only two words on that front—renewal or deportation. Any questions? Don't bother.

End of flashback. Music and lights cross fade from them to Jeena who is sitting quietly in her big family room. We hear Jeena's internal voice.

JEENA: And that's what we have got—A Family. What about freedom? I feel that I am caught in a circle going round and round and doing the same thing over and over. First I killed myself to buy this house and now I might die paying it off. I want to scream yet I don't know if anybody will hear me out in the cage I am in. Huh . . . the family is like an octopus with thousand tentacles. You escape from one and another grabs you. That's how I know it's my family.

QAISER: I pay the bills!

JEENA: They are on the table.

QAISER: Let's see. Hydro, telephone, t.v., gas . . .

JEENA: And property tax.

QAISER: Already.

JEENA: Don't forget insurance and school tax.

QAISER: Never ends.

JEENA: Like a master-slave relationship.

QAISER: Are you calling me the master?

JEENA: Home is our master. Furnish, care, watch, repair, maintain. A task for life.

A bag comes flying.

QAISER: Here fly in her books.

Samreen enters.

SAMREEN: Hi mom, hi baba.
QAISER: Where were you? It is quite late.
SAMREEN: Ma, I want to go to Toronto.
QAISER: For how long?
SAMREEN: For the weekend.
QAISER: Forget it.
SAMREEN: It is an educational trip.
QAISER: How much?
SAMREEN: I already got 100 working at the gallery.
QAISER: How much more.
SAMREEN: Two hundred.
QAISER: Too much.
SAMREEN: I will make do with 150.
JEENA: You will have two hundred.
QAISER: You spoil her.
JEENA: That's how we planned it dear. Not to have another child so we can give her our best and most.
JEENA: Thanks mom and dad. You saved me from being jealous.

Sound of a door bell.

QAISER: That must be Teja.
JEENA: Are you going somewhere with him?
QAISER: To a meeting.

Enters Teja.

JEENA: Assalam-walc-kum Teja.
TEJA: Sat-sri-akal ji.
QAISER: I better get dressed.

Qaiser Leaves.

SAMREEN: Uncle Teja, I know why you are dressed in your checkered jacket.

TEJA: Why?

SAMREEN: For the subsidized multicultural dinner.

TEJA: Somebody big is coming from Ottawa.

SAMREEN: A hand-shake day?

TEJA: It is different this time.

SAMREEN: That's novel. Is it election time already?

TEJA: It is constitution talk time.

SAMREEN: So this "somebody big" from Ottawa is going to pat your shoulders, "Canada is a community of communities."

TEJA: You know us ethnics. We have to be assured.

SAMREEN: By a bureaucrat in a reception hall! And there the East Indian people gather to catch up on the gossip. Whose daughter has run away with whom? Whose son is going out with a white girl? Who had his picture taken with the Minister of Multiculturalism!

TEJA: And talk about tax loop holes and mortgage rates.

SAMREEN: And listen to the priest—(*Imitating the Mullah*) "Our women must remain in purdah."

TEJA: (*Enjoying*) He is protecting women from other men.

SAMREEN: Women should be protected from him. The asshole says "our boys must not get trapped by impure white women. White women are not thoroughbreds. If our boys father a child with a white woman, they are ruining a centuries' old culture." Disgusting bloody old smut.

JEENA: Enough, Samreen.

SAMREEN: If his culture is so bloody fragile, why did he come here in the first place?

TEJA: To save enough and go back to his roots.

SAMREEN: Bloody hypocrite. If I ever hear him talk like that again, honest to God, I'll puncture his testicles.

JEENA: Samreen.

TEJA: Let's be honest Samreen. He gets hundreds of people for his weekly lectures.

SAMREEN: Which people and what lecture? Five hundred East Indian people telling other five hundred East Indian people what it is like to be East Indian in the western context?

TEJA: (*Jokingly*) I think you will understand that when baba finds a suitable match for you from India.

SAMREEN: No thank you, I am not interested in training an apprentice in integration.

JEENA: Enough Samreen.

Sound of a car horn.

TEJA: Who is that?

SAMREEN: No one.

TEJA: Where are you going?

SAMREEN: Library.

Samreen leaves in hurry.

TEJA: She means Talat.

JEENA: Yeah, I remember the look.

TEJA: Samreen is a smart girl.

JEENA: It's the boy I'm worried about.

TEJA: Talat is a good boy. And the family is good too.

JEENA: You never know these half Indian, half Canadians. They want the best of both worlds. I have seen so many immigrant sons do the same thing.

TEJA: You mean return back to their roots and marry a certified virgin?

Qaiser enters.

QAISER: Where did Samreen go?

TEJA: Library.

QAISER: Let us go. There are plenty of our people in this country. We should build contacts for our Dhaba.

JEENA: Qaiser, the doctor is coming today.

QAISER: What?

JEENA: You want me to repeat?

QAISER: Why do you invite people who. . . .

JEENA: Who do what?

QAISER: Never mind.

JEENA: I did not call her. She was driving by this way and wanted to drop by. She thinks the work is killing me and I must stop. She wants to talk to you too. What was I supposed to say? Please don't come.

QAISER: You don't need a doctor to convince me. If you want to stop, you don't need my permission. But there is a talk of strike in my factory.

JEENA: Strikes are happening all over these days.

QAISER: People are losing jobs all over too. In case you forget, we have a mortgage to pay.

TEJA: Big deal, you have a Dhaba to fall back on.

JEENA: Go and build contacts in the multicultural conference. I will explain to the doctor.

Teja and Qaiser leave. Lights converge on Jeena as we hear her internal voice.

JEENA: Lately the separatists are gearing up to their thing again. (*Sarcastically*) "Le Quebec aux quebecoise". I remember such slogans, back in India, the year we lost everything. If it wasn't for them, we wouldn't have fled our home, in the first place. And I wouldn't have been killing myself to make a home because we had a home back home. I want to grab hold of one of those separatists and shake him up, "do you know what you are doing? Look at me? This is what fleeing home has done to me? It is for people like you that a man has to run away with a brick in his hand?" Companies are closing all over since the separatists got active again. Then there is this strike that is dragging on in Qaiser's factory. Just a thought that I may be uprooted a second time in my life, frightens me to death.

Light out on Jeena, come up on the Dhaba. In The background pro and anti separatist slogans can be heard (vive le Quebec Libre. Quebec Yes, Canada No). Martin enters.

MARTIN: Marie-France, it is all over.

MARIE-FRANCE: The strike?

MARTIN: The company slammed the door on us after six weeks.

MARIE-FRANCE: What do you mean?

MARTIN: Declared bankruptcy. Just like that. You know there are lot of guys who have poured blood, sweat and tears into the factory. And just like that, all gone, not even a good bye.

Arrives Qaiser, throws his brief case on the counter.

QAISER: Are you happy now Martin?
MARTIN: Some of us didn't want to live in shit and feel great about it.
QAISER: It is stupid to go on strike when the economy is in a mess.
MARTIN: When is a good time to go on strike? When the economy is booming? Striking is all we had left for our pride.
QAISER: What pride are we going to experience lining up in front of the U.I. office?
MARIE-FRANCE: Makes you sick, doesn't it.
MARTIN: Do the politicians know about it.
MARIE-FRANCE: Do they care? I mean they have been locked up somewhere talking about constitution, they don't even remember there is a recession. One day one of them will need a screwdriver and get lost looking for Pascals.
TEJA: This English French thing is so stupid, you don't know which one will sell the other out before selling you out.
MARTIN: I bet our trouble started with this separatist thing.
MARIE-FRANCE: What more do the separatists want?
MARTIN: I think they want to separate.
TEJA: Good answer.
MARTIN: They want to bring Quebecoise babies in the world from the old stock Quebecoise.
MARIE-FRANCE: Everything of their own right down to the dirty movies. And all for them and them alone. So that Celine Dion wouldn't have to go to L.A.
MARTIN: But what am I going to do? Move out west? Or live on 250 dollar a week U.I.C. and 6 weeks of job retraining.
QAISER: What retraining? Who will hire a 50 year old man? I will be turned down wherever I go. It's so depressing.
TEJA: Don't worry, you will get used to it.
QAISER: What? Being depressed?
TEJA: No being turned down.

QAISER: You are so depressing.

TEJA: Qaiser, let's face it. You were manager in a third rate factory which hired cheap labour to work their 1970 model machines. But I guess you heard words like modernization, high tech, cost cutting and computer. My friend, your best bet is the Dhaba.

QAISER: Where will we get customers? Factory is closed. Dhaba will have to be folded too.

TEJA: If we fold up now, we may not have customers waiting when things get better.

QAISER: We may not have to fold up, if we had customers now.

TEJA: That is another catch 22. That is why I say it is time to move to a new location. Re-invest a 100 or couple of hundred thousand dollars. . . .

QAISER: Where will we get the money?

TEJA: Borrow! Use your house as collateral.

QAISER: Are you crazy? We still have a mortgage to pay off.

TEJA: That is why I am saying, don't condemn your lifelong struggle to futility. I am not begging for alms. I am making a business proposition.

Lights cross fade from Dhaba to the family home where we see Jeena sitting in a chair with a walking stick beside her. She looks unwell. We hear her internal voice. Qaiser and Samreen are seen in frozen postures, in the background under dim light.

JEENA: (*Internal*) Survival at all cost. Even Qaiser doesn't think about it—he believes in it. But I am running out of excuses. Excuses like—"so what? If it is not the disease, the age will stop me. Or what will Samreen do, as if she is helpless without me. And the recent one—the way factories are closing these days, it will be stupid to quit while they are still in business especially now that Qaiser's company has gone bankrupt. Too long I have convinced myself that all success stories are similar: all struggles are struggles in different ways." Not any more. Now I have begun to question. He wants to save his house at any cost. But how will I save my lungs and legs.

And there is this doctor Khaber! She keeps coming with new ways. Now she has begun to talk about suing the factory.

Door bell sounds as Qaiser breaks from his freeze. As he hears the door bell, he begins to rush out.

QAISER: I have to go out for a while.

JEENA: Qaiser stay. She wants to talk to you.

QAISER: Nobody told me.

SAMREEN: You didn't tell anybody that you had to go out.

QAISER: Is that how you talk to me?

JEENA: Qaiser, doctor Khaber is going to stay until you come back. So please open the door.

Qaiser opens the door. Enters Khaber.

KHABER: Hello, Mr. Quraishi. I am glad I found you home.

QAISER: Where could a jobless person go?

KHABER: Mr. Quraishi, I wanted to talk with you both. About Jeena. I have got some of the test results and I'm afraid the news isn't good.

SAMREEN: Oh no.

JEENA: I didn't think it would be.

QAISER: Yes, Jeena has been complaining for some time.

KHABER: Well, she hasn't quit yet, but I have been complaining for a long time.

SAMREEN: I have been begging her to quit.

QAISER: Samreen.

KHABER: She is showing signs of acute vascular clotting in her lower extremities and the X-ray suggests deposition of fibrous agents probably due to inhalation which might cause irreversible pulmonary damage.

QAISER: I only speak English and Urdu, doctor.

KHABER: I am recommending that she rests.

SAMREEN: It is about time.

QAISER: What?

SAMREEN: There is no 'what?' about it baba. Working under 30 degree heat with buzzing machines is no job for my sick mother.

JEENA: But it is better than *no job* at all.

KHABER: Jeena, I am ordering you to rest. No Work.

QAISER: That is fine, but you are scaring her.

KHABER: No, Mr. Quraishi I am doing my job. I am taking care of my patient.

SAMREEN: Thank you very much Khaber.

KHABER: Jeena, Now I have strong evidence that your injuries are related to your work. So with my letter you can stop the work without loss of your income for some months. In the meantime a few other doctors, social workers and lawyers will take legal action against the company on behalf of the victims.

JEENA: Victims?

SAMREEN: That includes you ma.

KHABER: Mind you most of them are immigrant women.

JEENA: What does it mean doctor?

KHABER: It means, if we win, and that is still a big if, you might collect some compensation.

JEENA: What will it compensate?

KHABER: Permanent injuries that the sweat factory gave you.

QAISER: Could it be substantial?

KHABER: My main concern is her health.

QAISER: Yes. Of course. Thank you very much doctor.

KHABER: But I want you to do some work for me Mr Quraishi. I want you to find this character Bernie.

QAISER: Why?

KHABER: Because, like Jeena some other women did piece work for him besides working in the factory.

SAMREEN: And you figure that the factory will try to establish that the piece work is responsible for the illness.

KHABER: A number of these women are from the same neighbourhood and like Jeena they all worked at homes.

SAMREEN: Implying that the conditions at home were hazardous?

KHABER: Yes and implying that the women brought illness upon themselves.

SAMREEN: Disgusting.

KHABER: So Jeena, are you ready?

JEENA: Ready for what?

KHABER: To sue the . . .

SAMREEN: . . . bastard factory owner.

QAISER: Samreen!

JEENA: Compensation is a silly word.

KHABER: Yes it is. It is a silly word. Nothing could compensate the injuries to your legs and lungs. But I had asked you to stop. Did you? Now I am asking you again. Compensation does sound silly, but it is your right. I am leaving these papers. Read them, think about it, sign and call me. I promised to visit two more women. Bye now.

Doctor Khaber leaves.

SAMREEN: Bye Khaber.
JEENA: Bye doctor.
QAISER: Thank you very much doctor.
JEENA: (*Softly*) Sure.
SAMREEN: I will find Bernie. I will go to my old neighbourhood.
QAISER: Teja will know. He brought him to us.
JEENA: (*Sarcastically*) Didn't waste any time. I had not written a letter back home and he was on my door with his sewing machine and rags.
QAISER: He has to be in the city. Because he left his machine downstairs . . . . just in case.
JEENA: (*Sarcastically*) As a souvenir. Every time I pass by, it buzzes in my ears. . . . What a bargain Teja had brought for me .....

Flashback: Sound of sewing machine resonates blending into flashback music taking us into the past, little after the family had arrived in Canada. Jeena in an empty room of her old apartment. Teja brings Bernie, who is carrying a sewing machine on his shoulders.

BERNIE: (*Annoying voice*) Hi. Are you Jeena? I know you are. Hi, I am Birny. I better slam down the machine on this table before I wreck my waist.

Bernie slams down the sewing machine on the table.

JEENA: I don't think I know you.
BERNIE: That just proves you are new in the neighbourhood.
TEJA: Bernie tell her about the bargain.
BERNIE: (*To Jeena*) You run my machine. I will lease it to you. I

bring the rag you sew the label. I deliver, I pick up and I pay you cash . . . No tax. And if you don't mind my saying, you will be sitting pretty with a deal like this because the more you work the more you get. You can build your future stacking up labels right here in the comfort of your home. (*Pause*) What's the matter? Don't you talk? Do you understand English? Eh? Speak French or what? Parle vous francaise?

JEENA: No Mr. Bernie, my country was colonized by the English.

BERNIE: Whatever that means. I don't care whether you speak English or French. I would prefer if you spoke neither.

JEENA: I prefer to go out and look for a job.

TEJA: But Jeena, where will you leave your one year old?

BERNIE: Listen lady, there is no shortage of your kind in Canada.

JEENA: (*To Teja*) What does he mean by that?

TEJA: You know . . . the runaways, . . . the boat people, . . . the aliens, the refugees you know.

BERNIE: And their women work for less.

TEJA: (*Patronizing, to Jeena*) Shit, I don't know why these refugees jump the boat and bring down the wages of senior refugees. I mean if they stayed home. . . . .

BERNIE: What would I do? Har har har . . . Just kidding. Look madam, if you have something else lined up, I will take my mobile business back. I haven't got all day.

TEJA: Jeena he hasn't got all day.

BERNIE: Look lady, I know why Teja and your hubby came to me. If a man wants to put jewellery and furs around his wife's neck, send his children to private school, own a Pontiac, a stationwagon and a boat and live in a brick house, he has got to work like a dog and make his wife work like a dog. So be a good girl, okay. I am going to show you how this machine works. Like this . . . pedal back and forth.

Bernie demonstrates how the machine works. Sound of machine blends with the music and brings us to the present. Jeena and Qaiser, in the family room.

QAISER: Jeena, Samreen has gone to look out for Bernie. She should be back soon.

JEENA: I know she has gone to look out for him.

QAISER: The factory should be sued for every single penny for doing this to you.

JEENA: The factory Qaiser?

QAISER: Didn't you hear the doctor? She sounds very confident that you will win.

JEENA: And also pay off your house.

QAISER: Our house.

JEENA: I just don't understand, what is in this house that I have abused myself so much. For what? The walls, the ceilings, the window, what? What about me?

QAISER: This is about you. Beside we can pay off the mortgage.

JEENA: Is that what I am worth? I don't want to live here anymore.

QAISER: Jeena, I understand you are upset. I am upset too. But if you sign. . . .

JEENA: How long have I been in this country?

QAISER: About twenty years.

JEENA: Not about twenty years. More than twenty years. And now I must depend on whether or not I find a man called Bernie.

QAISER: No Jeena, you must trust your doctor. Sign these.

JEENA: Compensation. What does she think I am? What do you think I am? Stuff of trade? Is that what I have to do? Trade my injuries to save his house? Answer me Qaiser.

QAISER: Don't scream.

JEENA: Answer. . . . .

QAISER: Jeena, if you think any wrong has been done to you for the house, the compensation is going to make up for it.

JEENA: Will it? Look at me. What will it make up for me? I don't even remember how I looked when I was younger? Am I the same? Is this me? (*She pulls her stiff & twisted fingers*) Is this my face, my hair? (*She scratches her face, pulls her hair*). Look at my belly?

Jeena beats herself.

QAISER: (*Screams*) Stop it. Stop it. Stop it . . .

JEENA: No this is not me.

Qaiser grabs Jeena's face with both his hands. Drags her by the mirror . . .

QAISER: You want a proof. Look into the mirror. That is you. Feel your face between my hand? That is your face. I am only trying to make best out of the situation. So stop acting mad. Sign the form and I will take it to the doctor when I come back from the Dhaba.

Jeena quietens down, Qaiser leaves her from his grab.

QAISER: (*Softly*) Please sign the form and I will take it to the doctor.

Qaiser leaves slamming the door.

JEENA: (*Sarcastically*) Please sign the form and I will take it to the doctor.

Samreen enters.

SAMREEN: Ma, what is wrong with baba. He was so uptight. Says the woman doesn't understand anything.
JEENA: Woman meaning me?
SAMREEN: (*Noticing her face*) Ma is everything okay? Are you alright ma.
JEENA: I am alright.
SAMREEN: You don't look okay.
JEENA: I don't know what to look like.
SAMREEN: Okay. Ma, I am sorry I didn't find Bernie.
JEENA: I didn't want you to.
SAMREEN: The women say they haven't seen him for some time but they suspect he is still in town.
JEENA: I didn't want you to go looking for him.
SAMREEN: Ma, it is not a small court claim settlement.
JEENA: I don't want it.
SAMREEN: You what?
JEENA: Don't you hear.
SAMREEN: Ma, you still make less than my summer job.
JEENA: I have made up my mind.

SAMREEN: You are sure you don't want to think it over. Least you could do for yourself is get paid for the damages.

JEENA: No. Funny—Now everybody is calling it a damage. Earlier it was called building the future. I want to tell you something Samreen.

SAMREEN: Let me get your medicine.

JEENA: No let me tell you.

SAMREEN: You can tell me while I apply medicine on your leg. Okay.

Samreen starts to apply a lotion on her mother's leg.

JEENA: Can you believe it happened for a brick.

SAMREEN: How many times I told you to stop, but you didn't.

JEENA: Let me tell you. I want you to hear it carefully. You had just started going to kindergarden. Which gave me hope that I will start my career as a teacher. But I couldn't stop the realities of the life cycle. Whether I wanted or not I had to make certain choices—for you, for your father and an authentic brick that meant everything to him. For him a man once dispossessed of his home would remain a man without identity unless he gets one. . . .

SAMREEN: That's all you have done. Made sacrifices.

JEENA: That's the story, and it goes on.

SAMREEN: And stupid me I never wondered why it is the same people who go on working in the factories.

JEENA: I still don't believe I worked 20 years in a factory that crippled me. And it happened for a brick.

SAMREEN: If it wasn't for the doctor you wouldn't stop.

JEENA: Samreen I am scared. I was scared like this only once before in my life. Back in India during the riots when masked men attacked me. And now when I am going cripple. I am beginning to hate myself for letting this happen to me.

SAMREEN: Why didn't you stop?

JEENA: That is a million dollar question. But I know I had to look after you.

SAMREEN: Look at you ma. You could not look after yourself. How do you think you were looking after me?

JEENA: That's how you will behave with me?

SAMREEN: Do you think I will enjoy the future you built for me on your injuries.

JEENA: I know I am not going to trade my injuries to build any future.

SAMREEN: You are sure you don't want to think it over one more time.

JEENA: Whatever is left of my life, I want to live the way I want to.

SAMREEN: Now you say that ma? Ma, I have inherited lots of things from you. But silence is not one of them. I think somebody will have an earful from me. Bye ma.

Flashback: As Samreen leaves, the sound of her fading footsteps blends in flashback music. We go in Jeena's mind as she recalls when Samreen was five. Jeena is working in her old apartment. Qaiser comes back from work and little Samreen is getting ready to go.

JEENA: Where are you going.

SAMREEN: To play.

JEENA: At Silvie's house?

SAMREEN: Why do you ask when you already know where I am going?

JEENA: Why don't you tell me before you make your plans?

SAMREEN: Who would I tell? You weren't home.

JEENA: Why didn't you tell your father?

SAMREEN: He is never home.

QAISER: When I come back from work, I want to see you home.

JEENA: And I want to see you eat my curry.

SAMREEN: When I come back from school nobody is home. When I go to play, both of you wait for me at home.

QAISER: This is what Canada does to children. If I talked to my father like that, he would have knocked some sense into my head.

JEENA: And if I insulted the curry like she does, my mother would have shoved some chicken curry down my throat.

SAMREEN: I don't like chicken.

JEENA: I cooked it fresh for you and it smells so good.

SAMREEN: It smells of curry.

QAISER: See how she insults the curry that made us world famous.

JEENA: There is a sandwich on the table.

SAMREEN: I don't want it. It has got cheese.

JEENA: What's wrong with the cheese?

SAMREEN: It has got holes in it.

JEENA: (*Frustrated*) Eat the cheese and leave the holes. Okay.

SAMREEN: Mama, Mrs. Thomson said you must come to the parent-teacher meeting.

QAISER: You eat your food.

SAMREEN: Mama did you hear what I said ?

JEENA: Yes I did.

SAMREEN: Why don't you answer then ?

JEENA: What don't I answer ?

SAMREEN: I am saying come to meet my teacher and you are telling me to eat curry.

QAISER: Eat and go to your room.

SAMREEN: Why do you stop me from going to Silvie's when you have to send me to my room.

JEENA: Because you are better off in your own home than at Silvie's.

SAMREEN : Then why can't I stay with both of you.

JEENA: You are staying with both of us.

SAMREEN: But baba said to go to my room.

QAISER: Because children should leave their parents alone sometimes.

SAMREEN: Is that why parents have children so they can leave them alone.

QAISER: Jeena make her eat before she goes to play.

JEENA: But I can't quarrel with her to feed her.

SAMREEN: Mama what is a quarrel?

JEENA: When you fight with someone without a weapon.

SAMREEN: A weapon?

JEENA: Weapon is what you fight with.

SAMREEN: Is daddy a weapon?

QAISER: What?

SAMREEN: You always quarrel for money to buy a house.

JEENA: Little chatterbox. She won't inherit my silence.

Sound of turning the keys is heard as the flashback ends and we come to the present. Jeena breaks out of her memories as Qaiser enters.

QAISER: Okay Jeena, on my way from the Dhaba, which is doing very bad, I stopped over at the bank to rearrange the mortgage payments. Because even with the rent coming from the tenants upstairs, installments are getting harder to pay.

JEENA: Qaiser, why do you bring out your violin now.

QAISER: I asked for an emergency loan and there are none even for the emergency. But the bank man did some calculations for me. Even if we sold our house at the going price, after usual deductions we will be at a loss of about 7,000.

JEENA: Sacrifices are always a loss.

QAISER: There is a way to cut the losses.

JEENA: Has the bank man told you how?

QAISER: We can stop paying the installment and let the bank take it over.

JEENA: I don't want to know.

QAISER: So I am saying what I am saying,-not because it makes me happy but with the thought that we can save our house if. . . . Well the doctor needs your signature in five days. She has a deadline.

JEENA: Another one of those things?

QAISER: What another one?

JEENA: Blackmail.

QAISER: What is blackmail about it. This house is all we have worked for.

JEENA: What about me?

QAISER: God, you are so aggravating. What about me, what about me, what about me? Is that all you care.

JEENA: Really?

Jeena laughs.

Flashback: her laughter blends into Qaiser's laughter as we go back in time, five years after their arrival in Canada. In his old apartment, Qaiser is happily talking to Teja. Jeena is nearby.

QAISER: (*Laughing*) I met the real estate genius today.

TEJA: Jeena, do you want to help your husband buy a house.

JEENA: Oh, my apologies, Teja, that I am not convincing enough. But I guess that's all I have been doing—helping him.

TEJA: I have some advice for you.

JEENA: Why not? When it comes to advice you are only next to God. You gave Qaiser one advice and he ended up with Mr. Banks. Gave me another advice and I got Uncle Bernie. There must be some better advice somewhere.

TEJA: That's the next advice I was going to give you.

JEENA: I am waiting.

TEJA: I have a real job lined up for you.

JEENA: So I can say bye bye to the piece work?

TEJA: You shouldn't. Since women are paid only half the wages, you should do two jobs.

JEENA: And may I ask what is this job?

TEJA: A friend of mine has connections in the sweat factory.

JEENA: That's what Canada has become to us—a big Factory.

TEJA: I know you want to be a teacher. But let me tell you what you are up against. When you apply for a teaching job, only two things could happen. You want to know what? Either they will reject you flatly or recommend you to an evaluation committee. If it is rejection, well, the case is closed. But if it is the evaluation committee, only two things could happen. Either the evaluation committee will sit on your application or forward it to a higher committee. If they sit on your application well, good luck. But if it is the higher committee, only two things can happen. Either they will send it back to the first committee or send it to the next committee. If it is the first committee, well let's start all over again. But if it is the next committee, only two things could happen. Either they will ask you to take a proficiency exam or call for an interview. If it is the interview watch your accent. But if it is the proficiency exam, only two things could happen. Either you pass or fail. If you fail well chapter closed. But if you pass, only two things will happen. Either they will ask you to present the original transcript, which you can't present because they are burnt to ashes, or be put on a waiting list until the facts are established some other way so that you could become a substitute teacher in some elementary school. And then you are going to say you could have helped your husband better by working in a factory than being on the waiting list. Now if you still want to try something new, remember, you will have to start from scratch and only two things could happen. You want me to go on?

JEENA: This is a blackmail.

TEJA: But there is a certain logic to it.

JEENA: It sure is. (*Sarcastic laugh*)

Laughter blends/fades as we come back to the present, with Qaiser and Jeena, in their new house.

JEENA: So what's your logic now.

QAISER: No blackmail, but the deadline is in five days. That's why I have to find Bernie for you, because if I didn't find him, the doctor's struggle will be futile and you might not win. And if you don't win, the factory will not re-hire you when you get well. So while I go on trying to search for Bernie, you have five days to sign the papers.

JEENA: And you said, no blackmail.

QAISER: I said I want to save the house.

Qaiser leaves, musical interlude as Jeena walks around the house aimlessly. Five days later, at the Quraishi home, Samreen enters.

SAMREEN: Ma, are you alright?

JEENA: (*Startled*) You gave me a fright.

SAMREEN: Ma you are very quiet.

JEENA: I have been doing some thinking on my own.

Qaiser walks in.

QAISER: Jeena, I am heading out to the doctor's office.

SAMREEN: Baba, she has already said, she is not signing.

QAISER: Samreen I am not talking to you.

SAMREEN: But you are talking about my mother.

QAISER: And you are talking in my house.

SAMREEN: Baba, why don't you listen to anyone for once. Sell this stupid house. Move to an apartment which we can afford without trading her injuries.

QAISER: Where do you get the idea that Jeena will be better off in an apartment than in a house.

SAMREEN: Baba, I think you don't listen. Ma has made up her mind.

QAISER: Listen young lady. I don't need some 21 year old to tell me what to do?

SAMREEN: She is my mother.

QAISER: She is my wife.

JEENA: My mother, my wife, your mother, your wife, does anybody want to talk to Jeena. I came here to live and all I have done is work, work, and work. And now the doctor is blaming me for my own injuries. I will be a prisoner of my own faults for the rest of my life.

QAISER: What faults?

JEENA: Qaiser we didn't come here to get rich. We came here because the fanatics chased us out as traitors. Since then we have been trying to build our house in this country. And that's all we have done. Build, build and build. We were so busy building the house that I did not even have time to live in it. I am going cripple. Soon I will be locked in some rest home for the rest of my life. Who will shed tears for me? And now you want me to trade my injuries so that you can save your house.

QAISER: That's what you think of me? Hah.

SAMREEN: Baba, ma is trying to communicate something to you.

QAISER: You listen to me young lady. From the very day I set my foot in this country, they called me a run-away, an alien, boat people, and the latest one—an allophone. Do you think it has been easy for me. I also have scars on my back. That's what I had to do for this house. Do you think I will let it go just because Jeena will not sign a piece of paper.

SAMREEN: What are you going to do?

QAISER: I could do it all over again.

JEENA: What are you going to trade, Qaiser?

QAISER: You watch and see.

SAMREEN: Baba where are you going?

QAISER: Out.

Qaiser slams door and leaves. We hear car start and leave.

JEENA: Samreen, bring those papers the doctor left for me to sign.
SAMREEN: But you said you are not signing.
JEENA: But I didn't say I am.
SAMREEN: Are you playing games ma?
JEENA: Bring the papers.
SAMREEN: I think everybody is going bonkers.

Lights out on them. Lights come up on the Dhaba. Qaiser arrives at the Dhaba.

QAISER: Teja, where are you?
TEJA: You look angry brick man.
QAISER: Don't you call me brick man.
TEJA: Sorry brick man.
QAISER: (*Loud, angry*) I said don't call me brick man.
TEJA: What's the matter? The wife giving trouble.
QAISER: Teja, what is the name of this Dhaba?
TEJA: What's wrong with you today.
QAISER: How come it is Teja's Tandoori Dhaba? How come it is not Qaiser and Teja's Tandoori Dhaba.
TEJA: Are you drunk? I am scrambling to get customers and you are crying about your name.
QAISER: I won't have to because I want to pull out from the business.
TEJA: You are what?
QAISER: You heard me.
TEJA: Without consulting me?
QAISER: When did you consult me?
TEJA: I made you a 50-50 partner when you needed credit, confidence and contacts.
QAISER: You needed my savings to invest in the Dhaba.
TEJA: So you can use the Dhaba as collateral to get mortgage. And I let you do your regular job while I minded the Dhaba. I helped you when you needed help. Now you are leaving me when things aren't going good.
QAISER: You talk like you are my wife. My decision is strictly busi-

ness.

TEJA: Qaiser, the partnerships are based on trust.

QAISER: So?

TEJA: You are betraying it.

QAISER: I am only human.

TEJA: So our entire investment goes to waste. Just like that.

QAISER: That sums up the fate of an immigrant business. You told me Canada will teach me some of life's hard realities. Well I have to prove some realities to my family.

Qaiser looks deep into Teja's eyes and opens the business papers in front of him. Lights go out on them. Lights come back on at the home. Qaiser enters his home.

QAISER: (*Calling loud*) Jeena. Jeena. Where are you?

Enters Samreen.

SAMREEN: Welcome to the museum of mama's sacrifices.

QAISER: Don't talk nonsense. Where is she?

SAMREEN: When I saw her last she was sitting with your favourite brick. Then she said she was going for a walk.

QAISER: Now what is she waiting for? A grand entrance? You go get her. Right away. (*Pause*) Why aren't you saying anything?

SAMREEN: (*Shattered*) Baba, she is not coming back to this house.

QAISER: What? I am up to my neck with her irrationality. Where is she?

SAMREEN: Baba . . .

QAISER: (*Loud, ordering*) Where is she?

SAMREEN: (*Choking*) Baba, she has signed the papers as you wanted her to.

QAISER: I don't need her signatures—not for me not for my house. I know how to make sacrifices too. I just sold my share in the Dhaba. Where is she? I want to tell her that.

SAMREEN: She left a letter for you. (*Starts sobbing*)

QAISER: Letter? What for?

SAMREEN: It is under the brick.

Qaiser goes by the brick. Picks up the letter.

QAISER: Where is she? Which corner has she chosen to brood this time? Samreen, why don't you answer me? How come you are silent? . . . . Where is your mother? Jeena, Jeena. . . .

SAMREEN: (*Crying, loud*) Baba, ma has left. She is not coming back.

Lights narrow on the brick as stage blacks out.

COUNTER OFFENCE

Acknowledgements: This play was written and developed with the financial assistance of the *Canada Council*. Help was also received from the *Cahoots Theatre Projects* and from the *Ontario Arts Council*. Counter Offence was workshopped at the *Playwrights Workshop Montreal*, with the participation of actors from *Teesri Duniya Theatre* company which also produced the play in Montreal.

Shazia, daughter of East Indian immigrant parents, marries Shapoor, an Iranian on a student visa. She sponsors him for Canadian resident status. While the process drags on, their marriage takes an ugly turn. Shapoor hits Shazia and she calls in the police. Sgt Galliard attends Shazia's call and temporarily arrests Shapoor.

Mr. Moolchand Misra, an anti-racist activist and a family friend accuses Sgt. Galliard of racial misconduct against Shapoor. Moolchand questions cultural sensitivity of Montreal cops.

On the other hand, Ms Clarinda Keith, a black social worker, fully committed to zero-tolerance on violence against women, comes to Galliard's defence.

However, Mr Moolchand manages to put Sgt. Galliard through an inquiry. This angers the police brotherhood, who regard the inquiry as an offence against entire police force.

Meanwhile Shazia decides to end her marriage with Shapoor, which results in his deportation.

But Shapoor returns back only to be found shot dead in his YMCA hotel room. He was a wife beater and a deportee but now he is dead. Everybody is a suspect.

Did Shapoor's race affect Sgt Galliard's judgement? If so, how did Shazia's race affect Galliard's conduct? *Counter Offence* explores an explosive situation when crime against a woman is turned into a crime against race.

CHARACTERS

Shazia Rizvi:	A 26 year old Muslim woman brought up in Canada
Shapoor Farhadi:	Her Iranian husband who came to Canada as a student
Clarinda Keith:	A black woman who runs a centre for battered women
Guy Galliard:	Police officer who works in the domestic unit
Gilles Prougault:	President of the police brotherhood (union)
Moolchand Misra:	An "Indo Canadian"—an anti-racist activist
Mohammed Murad Rizvi:	Shazia's father. Retired. He is from India
Shafiqa Rizvi:	Shazia's mother, a good woman who speaks frankly and without fear

Counter Offence was first produced by *TEESRI DUNIYA THEATRE* at the Strathearn Intercultural Centre, Montreal, from March 14-31, 1996. The cast and crew was as follows:

Shazia Rizvi	Raminder Singh
Shapoor Farhadi	Cas Anvar
Clarinda Keith	Judy Rudd
Guy Galliard	Stephen Orlov
Gilles Prougault	Mark Walker
Moolchand Misra	Prasun (raja) Lala
Mohammed Murad Rizvi	Kapil Bawa
Shafiqa Rizvi	Ranjana Jha

Director	Jack Langedijk
Set and Light design	J. David Gutman
Music	Raiomond Mirza
Costume	Rossana Higgins
Stage Manager	James Douglas
Poster design	Raminder Singh
Production Manager	Jim Patrick
Publicity	Jonathan McKiel

COUNTER OFFENCE

The set consists of a family home, a women's shelter, a police station and a neutral acting area. All the above serve multiple purpose. There are four doorframes which can be moved around the stage. By laying them horizontally they become a table, a railing or a platform.

Downstage right, is Rizvie's house—symbolized by a bed, a small table, a telephone and a tel directory. East Indian decoration hangs from the ceiling. The house will also be used as a YMCA hotel room by changing the configuration of the bed.

Downstage left is a women's shelter which also acts as Clarinda's office. It has a table, a chair, and a small stool.

Another stool is located downstage centre.

At a certain point in the play, towards front of the stage, a detention cell will be represented by shadows of jail-bars falling on the floor.

Upstage is a police station situated on a riser. One doorframe will stay there permanently.

At the beginning of the play, the three movable doorframes are placed, one behind the other. They will be rearranged as the play proceeds.

For the most part, actors don't leave the stage. When a scene is underway, other actors remain frozen in abstract formations, under dim lights. They break from their freeze to act their parts when required. Time and place transitions as well as flashbacks are shown by changing lights.

Throughout the play, the courtroom is represented by a bright spotlight, from where the characters talk to an imaginary judge. The courtroom location changes from scene to scene.

(*NB: In the script, the courtroom is referred as "Courtroom Spotlight."*)

As the house lights fade out, actors walk in. Moolchand enters talking to the audience as other actors rearrange the doorframes. One doorframe is moved to be the women's shelter, one to be the family home and the third one stays center stage.

Lights brighten a bit. We see Prougault standing under the doorframe by the police-station while Galliard is under the doorframe located center-stage. Other actors stand still at various sites of the stage.

MOOLCHAND: I speak to you for a just cause, not because a young ethnic is being thrown out of the country, but because I'm driven by a social justice that thrives in this city. God knows, I'm doing something that our ancestors could not do, when they stepped on the soil of Canada. Komagatamaru, the Chinese head tax, native babies being taken away from their families, spouses kept apart right after their marriage because of the so-called immigration backlog. History that can't be rewritten, but hopefully guide us to a future that can. I'm not fighting against racism, I'm fighting for equality. Where police identify people by their acts and not by their skin. I'm fighting for a Canada that accepts what it is, a multi-ethnic society. I heard somebody say the other day that just like all ethnics, I am in the habit of putting down Canada. No sir, I chose Canada, this very city to be my home and all I'm trying to do is make my home better for my children, where I hope that some day we will focus on values rather than the colour of skin.

Lights fade-in a bit more on actors.

PROUGAULT: Will the defendant please rise, Guy Galliard, you stand accused of the murder of Shapoor Farhadi.

ALL ACTORS: (*Repeating*) I swear to tell the truth, the whole truth, and nothing but the truth. I swear to tell the truth, the whole truth and nothing but the truth. I swear to tell the truth, the whole truth and nothing . . .

Lights out on stage. Courtroom spotlight appears on Sgt. Galliard who is standing under the centre stage doorframe.

GALLIARD: (*In spotlight*) No, it's the God damn truth!—excuse me your Honour, but I have said the same thing every time. What sir? Shapoor called me—at my home, . . . We talked for a short time. I don't know, 5 minutes, . . . no not even 3—I went to his room at the YMCA. I remember the door was slightly open.

Flashback: courtroom spotlight out. Lights fade-in on the YMCA room where Shapoor is seen lying (dead) on the bed. Galliard walks over to his room.

GALLIARD: Shapoor ? . . . Shapoor !

He walks over to the dead body, moves it—it falls to the floor.

Oh shit, Oh, oh . . . (*He looks around the room*) . . . What the . . . (*Shakes him*) Come on you can't be . . .

In walks Shazia, she gasps, as she sees her husband lying on the floor and Galliard standing over him.

SHAZIA: What are you doing here?
GALLIARD: He called, . . . I . . . I . . . I don't know . . . he is dead.
SHAZIA: What? . . . What ? . . . My God . . . Shapoor . . .

She runs to him, holds his body in her arms.

Shapoor, Shapoor . . . Oh please, no . . . no . . . Oh my God. Please, . . . Shapoor, look at me, please, I'm sorry, too. Shapoor come on . . .

GALLIARD: (*Leans over Shazia's shoulders*) It's alright . . .
SHAZIA: (*Screams*) Get away, don't touch us. . . . Oh my Shapoor, (*To Galliard*) Get out, get out . . .

Galliard leaves. Lights fade-out on the YMCA. Galliard returns back to the courtroom spotlight.

GALLIARD: (*In the spotlight*) Yes, I did, I did your Honour, I called 911 but he was gone though, . . . I mean dead when I got there.

(*Pause, he listens*) No, ...Yes I did arrest Mr. Shapoor, seven months ago. But that doesn't mean that I . . . Your Honour, he won't even let me finish. Fine . . . yes, seven months ago, that was the first time I ever met him.

Flashback: Shapoor in dimly lit detention cell. Shadow of the jail bar can be seen on the floor. Galliard interrogating Shapoor.

SHAPOOR: Please, let me go. . . . Why have you brought me here? Please, let me go home.
GALLIARD: Home?
SHAPOOR: I want to know how is she doing?
GALLIARD: Shut up. (*Shapoor moves*) . . . Don't turn around.
SHAPOOR: Sir, you can't keep me here. Please, I need to get back home.
GALLIARD: To Aairan? No? No, you're going to sit here and you are going to tell me exactly what you did.
SHAPOOR: (*Mutters in Persian*) What more can I tell, I have told you every thing. I need to call my friend. Please just let me. . . .

Shapoor takes a step.

GALLIARD: Stop right there. (*Shapoor shocked*) . . .'N don't bloody shine your eyes on me. . . . Now very slowly, turn around, . . . don't even blink boy. Are you sure you don't have anything more to say? That's it? Put your hands behind your head, (*Shapoor turns towards him, Galliard shouts*) I said don't come near me, . . . Walk out that door, head back to the cell, nice and slow. . . .
SHAPOOR: This is insulting.
GALLIARD: Shut up.

Galliard pushes Shapoor out. Lights brighten on police station, where Prougault is busy writing a report. Galliard joins Prougault.

GALLIARD: Guys like him are scum, no better than pimps and child molesters.
PROUGAULT: (*Holding the report*) What does this say?
GALLIARD: (*Spells it*) A i i r a fucking "n" —Born in Aiiran.

PROUGAULT: (*Without paying attention*) Okay, so what's it gonna be? Disorderly conduct?

GALLIARD: Assault.

PROUGAULT: Oh yeah? (*Takes the photo from the file*) I am looking at the photo, I don't see any bruise 'n, blood 'n broken bone. Where is the doctor's report?

GALLIARD: (*Snatching the photo from him*) He's already confessed!

PROUGAULT: Guy, don't waste your time on minor matters.

GALLIARD: You need a damned seminar on wife assault.

PROUGAULT: You need a seminar on how things work around here. You can't lock him up on this.

GALLIARD: Sir this is not his first time, check the . . .

PROUGAULT: There is a thing called restraining order.

GALLIARD: How many ladies have been saved by a restraining order? Come on, he will be out gunning for her and he damn well knows where she lives.

PROUGAULT: That's when you lock him up.

GALLIARD: What? When she's dead?

PROUGAULT: Sergeant, if you put him away, for a little thing like this, he will come out even madder than before he went in.

GALLIARD: Oh, you give me a black eye, but I can't lock you up, even though I know you'll whack me again.

PROUGAULT: O.K. Guy, I guess you know your job better than I do. Where is the wife?

Lights go out on police station as courtroom spotlight appears on Clarinda who is standing under the doorframe by the women's shelter.

CLARINDA: (*In spotlight*) It's impossible, I can't believe Shazia could or would kill him. She was no different than any other woman . . . in her situation. The man did beat her. Mad? Of course she was mad But I really believe she was willing to forgive.

Flashback: Clarinda's office. She's counselling Shazia who is seen sitting on a stool with her back to the audience. Galliard is also present.

SHAZIA: I had to call the police.

CLARINDA: You could have waited until it was too late.

SHAZIA: I can't believe he hit me again!

CLARINDA: Again?

GALLIARD: Yes in the report . . .

CLARINDA: Thank you officer. I am sorry Shazia—please. . . .

SHAZIA: Well, not like this. . . . A month ago he threw hot coffee on my face.

GALLIARD: (*Under his breath*) Shit . . .

CLARINDA: . . . Sergeant!!

SHAZIA: I was so insulted, . . . so embarrassed.

CLARINDA: Didn't you tell anyone?

SHAZIA: No, I feel so little.

GALLIARD: You don't have to sweetheart. (*To Clarinda*) It's okay. (*To Shazia*) You don't have anything to feel ashamed about. You haven't done anything wrong. He has.

SHAZIA: What will happen to him?

CLARINDA: Don't worry.

SHAZIA: Where is he?

GALLIARD: He's locked up.

CLARINDA: Please Sergeant, will you excuse us now? Don't worry Shazia, Sgt Galliard will make sure . . .

SHAZIA: (*Runs up to the door as Galliard exits*) Don't let him out! Please don't let him. (*To Clarinda*) They won't let him out will they? Don't let . . .

CLARINDA: They won't. Not this time.

Murad and Shafiqa enter. They meet Galliard as he is heading back to the police station.

SHAFIQA: Thank you sir, thank you for saving our daughter.

MURAD: Thank you sir.

GALLIARD: It's alright, she is in. . .

MURAD: I never approved of that man.

GALLIARD: Don't worry, he won't hurt . . .

SHAFIQA: Thank you.

GALLIARD: Don't worry, he will never.

MURAD: Where is he?

GALLIARD: He's locked up. Your daughter's down the hall in that room.

SHAFIQA: Do you have him? (*Galliard nods*) Don't let him out!

Lights fadeout on them. Courtroom spotlight appears on Murad who has walked over to the doorframe by the women's shelter. Shafiqa stands nearby in dim light.

MURAD: (*In spotlight, to the imaginary judge*) He deserved to die. I am sorry your honour but Sgt Galliard, he had saved her once. He probably was doing the same. What? I don't care if he did call him camel breath. He could call me a paki a thousand times—if it would save my daughter. . . .

Flashback: courtroom spotlight out as lights come up on Clarinda's office. Murad steps out of the doorframe and walks over to her office. Shafiqa joins in. Clarinda continues to counsel Shazia like in the last scene.

SHAZIA: Options?

CLARINDA: None of us are ever prepared for a thing like this. (*Looking at file*) Now, you're the bread winner in the family?

SHAZIA: He just graduated.

SHAFIQA: To his fist?

MURAD: He sits home doing nothing while you pay the bills.

SHAFIQA: . . .While he moans about his carpet business.

SHAZIA: Ma! . . . (*To Clarinda*) His father sent him carpets from Iran. But he needs a loan to start a business. (*Spilling her hidden anger*) But if his father tells him to sell carpets, he will sell carpets, whether he wants to or not. The carpets are lying on some dock right now. Fool of a son of a fool of a father. If his father says go jump in a well, he will bloody well go jump in a well. He is cooking up a business like a fool in an Iranian folk tale, . . . pot hanging from the tree and candlelight on the ground.

MURAD: And she's left to fix the screw-ups!!

CLARINDA: Thank you, Shazia do you want your parents here?

SHAZIA: Yeah, it's okay. (*To her parents, in Hindi*) Thodi der ke liye jaban pay tala laga sakte hain? Please!!

SHAFIQA: Sorry, —go on doctor.

CLARINDA: So you refused to co-sign a loan for him?

SHAZIA: He can't get a loan on his own until his immigration is complete. Only God knows how long will that take. And . . . he has already. . . . He has already added his father and mother on the list.

MURAD: Mobsters!

SHAFIQA: They want a visa in dowry!

MURAD: Bloody criminals!

CLARINDA: What list?

SHAZIA: He went ahead and sponsored his parents even before his own visa is final. I'm broke, and he added two more dependents for me. I just can't. I have my parents here already. I can't.

CLARINDA: He didn't ask you first?

SHAZIA: No! That's how he always pisses me off. I 'm sorry.

SHAFIQA: No, don't worry, it's O.K.

CLARINDA: I understand.

SHAZIA: I just can't handle any more . . . I have my parents here . . .

MURAD: Are we a burden?

SHAFIQA: She's not saying that.

MURAD: Are we a burden? (*To Clarinda*) Doctor, we are waiting till our son . . . he lives in Vancouver. . .

SHAZIA: Abbu, please, I am only saying . . .

MURAD: That we are a burden.

SHAFIQA: She is not saying that. And if you think you are, . . . shut up and don't burden any more.

SHAZIA: Ammi, abbu, chup ho jaiye na please.

MURAD: Please doctor go on.

CLARINDA: Well Shazia, I should tell you what your options are.

SHAFIQA: Yes please.

CLARINDA: We can order mediation, order him counselling and/or you can take him back. . . .

SHAFIQA: What?

MURAD: What do you mean?

SHAFIQA: These are options?

SHAZIA: I am not sure.

CLARINDA: You are not sure of what?

MURAD: That we are a burden?

SHAZIA: I am not sure if I want him back any more.
MURAD: Oh!
CLARINDA: Are you sure?
SHAZIA: I am not sure if I am sure.
CLARINDA: There is something else you can do.
SHAZIA: What?
SHAFIQA: Yes doctor, please . . .
CLARINDA: You can withdraw his sponsorship.
MURAD: You mean immigration sponsorship? Half way through?
CLARINDA: It's a sure way of getting him out of your life.
SHAZIA: Pardon me?
CLARINDA: Deporting him.
MURAD: Good riddance, I never liked that fellow.
SHAZIA: Send him out of the country? That isn't right.
CLARINDA: What's right? Get beat up and live like a lame duck? Look, many men, . . . bring a bride from "home back home," beat her up and if she complains, blackmail her into sending her back . . . "back home". I see no reason why you can't do the same. I'm not suggesting that's what you should do. I 'm telling you that is one thing you can do.
MURAD: Yes, that's what she will do, doctor.
SHAFIQA: That's right, thank you doctor.
MURAD: Yes, that's a good option Doctor.
CLARINDA: Thank you, but I 'm not a doctor.
SHAZIA: When must I decide?
CLARINDA: Shazia, my motto is zero tolerance. My concern is with you, not him.
SHAZIA: But if I don't do this, do I have to live with him?
CLARINDA: Do you think he will leave you alone? (Silence) . . . I don't think so.

Lights fade out on them and come up on the police station. The upstage doorframe is lowered horizontally to act as a table where Prougault is busy completing a file. Moolchand enters.

PROUGAULT: Can I help you?
MOOLCHAND: If you don't mind helping a coloured man?
PROUGAULT: (*Visibly bothered but in humorous tone*) Try me.

MOOLCHAND: I want to see a man by the name of Shapoor Farhadi.

PROUGAULT: The guy from Iran?

MOOLCHAND: That's right, the guy from Iran.

PROUGAULT: Your client assaulted his wife.

MOOLCHAND: Come on, you are talking like a judge, as though my man is already proven guilty.

PROUGAULT: What's your name?

MOOLCHAND: Moolchand, Mr. Moolchand. Shapoor called me? What would you say is your name?

PROUGAULT: Gilles Prougault.

MOOLCHAND: The president of the Police Brotherhood?

PROUGAULT: Yeah.

MOOLCHAND: Lovely symbolism. Union, solidarity, brother . . . (*Stops, thinks and says. . .*) *Hood.* Hoods, I like that . . .

PROUGAULT: What do you want?

MOOLCHAND: What were we talking about? Shapoor, Mr. President, so what are you going to do with Shapoor?

PROUGAULT: I don't know, arrest him, walk the guy around the block. Mediate. But you might have a problem, the arresting officer feels your client should be locked up.

MOOLCHAND: A white officer?

PROUGAULT: (*With a deep breath*) Would you like to see him now?

MOOLCHAND: You didn't take that personally, did you Mr. Prougault? But you have to agree with me that a large number of citizens are uncomfortable with the way white officers treat other people.

PROUGAULT: Other people?

MOOLCHAND: Non-whites? People from other countries, cultures, traditions and histories.

PROUGAULT: Mister, . . .

Lights fade out on Prougault. In a rapid transition, Moolchand moves a step away as courtroom spotlight appears on him.

MOOLCHAND: (*In spotlight*) I thought the white people always bring up their past. They are always telling you how their ancestors fought a war in a coloured country. (*As though he is reminded by the judge*) . . . Yes your honour, Mr. Prougault seemed quite nervous when I introduced myself. Nervous? Yes like always hiding something from you? I cannot believe that I had to put my trust in men like him. . . .

Flashback: courtroom spotlights go out, lights come up on police station. Moolchand and Prougault talking in the police station.

PROUGAULT: You mean you're not his lawyer?
MOOLCHAND: Will it help you if I said that I . . . (*Smile, pause*) I am a member of the race tribunal.
PROUGAULT: Alright, (*Calling*) Shapoor Farhadi.

Shapoor enters.

MOOLCHAND: Shapoor!
SHAPOOR: Mr. Moolchand, please help me.
MOOLCHAND: I will. Excuse us. (*He takes Shapoor aside*) Sit down, What happened?
SHAPOOR: I don't know. . . I uh . . .uh . . .
MOOLCHAND: Where is she?
SHAPOOR: I don't know.
MOOLCHAND: Is there anything you do know?
SHAPOOR: I don't know. The police came and I am here. The last time . . .
MOOLCHAND: Shapoor, you have been here before?
SHAPOOR: Yes. That time, we just talked to some woman and . . . Shazia and I just went home. Oh, Mr. Moolchand . . .
MOOLCHAND: Why are you in jail now? Why should an East Indian wife behave in such a strange way?
SHAPOOR: I slapped her.
MOOLCHAND: You should not have.
SHAPOOR: Oh God, I know, oh God.
MOOLCHAND: What did she do?
SHAPOOR: She said insulting things about my father.
MOOLCHAND: Why?
SHAPOOR: I don't know! . . . I don't know.

MOOLCHAND: I thought mothers and fathers sent their children to Canada to know everything. Shapoor, I'm sorry, I can't help you. (*Starts to exit*)

SHAPOOR: (*Stands up*) Come on, you know my father has put me in a fix.

MOOLCHAND: (*Looking at Prougault*) Its alright Mr. Prougault. [*To Shapoor*] The carpets.

SHAPOOR: They're already on the dock. 100,000 dollars worth of Persian carpets.

MOOLCHAND: I told you to advise your father that we have rules in Canada.

SHAPOOR: I tried, and my wife advised him too. But then I got back on the phone and he said, "Son, what kind of man have you become? Is your wife going to advise me or are you going to tell her to listen?" I tried Mr. Moolchand, I tried to tell her . . . and here I am. And if I . . . .

MOOLCHAND: . . . And if you anger your father, he'll have a heart attack. Then, your mother will tell you—"Son, do you want to disgrace your father by disobeying him so that he has his heart attack now instead of later."

SHAPOOR: It's not a joke! He really does have a heart problem.

MOOLCHAND: This is more interesting than Aladdin and his carpets. Shapoor alright—Didn't you take care of what we talked about? Do you have a place to store them? A licence to sell them? Did you manage the loan?

SHAPOOR: No, my wife won't . . .

MOOLCHAND: What? Brilliance like that could only have come from a Concordia graduate. Now I understand why your wife must have thrown a fit. You know what will happen? Your carpets are going to rot on the docks and then they'll be auctioned off.

SHAPOOR: I wish I could just send them back. I need to talk to Shazia.

MOOLCHAND: Not many people have an eccentric father who is willing to stuff a business with a 500% profit potential down his son's throat.

SHAPOOR: Can you get me out of here?

MOOLCHAND: I could have if you hadn't hit your wife.

SHAPOOR: (*Almost in tears*) Oh God, if my father finds out about this . . .

MOOLCHAND: (*Pause*) Did the cop rough you up?

SHAPOOR: What?

MOOLCHAND: (*Whispers*) Did he make the crime you committed, the fault of your race or your culture? You know you being Iranian?

SHAPOOR: I hit her.

MOOLCHAND: You have already said that. You hit your wife. It should not happen, but it did. Now, did the cop treat you the same way he would have treated, . . . say a white person?

SHAPOOR: I don't know, he said some . . .

Lights fade out on them. We are back to the present time. Courtroom spotlight appears on Galliard who is now standing under the doorframe by Clarinda's office.

GALLIARD: (*In spotlight*) It was like it didn't matter what he did—but what I said. I am not a racist, I treat all wife beaters equally.

Courtroom spotlight out on Galliard and appears on Clarinda who is standing near her office.

CLARINDA: (*In spotlight*) No! She didn't kill him. I'm sorry your Honour, When I first heard of accusations of Shazia killing her husband, I almost believed it. He never really seemed honest and if she did kill . . .

Flashback: lights come up on the police station where Moolchand has come to free Shapoor. Clarinda walks over to the station from her courtroom spot. Moolchand heads towards Clarinda.

MOOLCHAND: I expected to see somebody black and blue.

CLARINDA: Sorry just black.

MOOLCHAND: No, no. what I meant was, I was expecting to see Shazia with you.

SHAPOOR: Is she here?

CLARINDA: She decided she can't face her tormentor under the circumstances. (*Starts to exit*)

MOOLCHAND: Ms, Ms, (*Moolchand pulls her aside*) . . . from what I hear, Shazia is not even bruised.

CLARINDA: She doesn't have to be.

MOOLCHAND: You're quite right. But, . . . But don't you think that's good reason why these children should forgive and forget the whole thing.

CLARINDA: Is that what you wanted to tell her?

SHAPOOR: No. . . .

MOOLCHAND: No Madame, I wanted to say he'll apologize to her in front of me and you.

SHAPOOR: I am really sorry. I am. I admit it.

CLARINDA: Is that it?

SHAPOOR: But, but . . .

MOOLCHAND: A good man sometimes makes a mistake and a good woman must forgive.

SHAPOOR: Yes, tell her to forgive me.

CLARINDA: Tell her?

MOOLCHAND: Does this look like the face of a wife beater to you?

CLARINDA: Is this his real face?

MOOLCHAND: Madam . . .

CLARINDA: Clarinda Keith.

MOOLCHAND: Ms Clarinda, I understand you. In fact I agree with you.

CLARINDA: Don't patronize me.

MOOLCHAND: I am not. I too have a problem with men like him, . . . they give a bad name to us. I can't even believe he did it. You know, we joke about him because in his everyday life, he is so docile, so domesticated, . . . he is pretty liberated for an Iranian, you know.

CLARINDA: So liberated that he hit her because she wouldn't take out a loan for his carpet business.

MOOLCHAND: They are a family!

CLARINDA: She doesn't want to be his family any more.

MOOLCHAND: What do you mean?

CLARINDA: She's decided to end the marriage.

SHAPOOR: She said this?

CLARINDA: She's withdrawing his sponsorship.

SHAPOOR: No. She said this? Please, no.
MOOLCHAND: It's alright Shapoor, . . . Ms Clarinda . . .
CLARINDA: She is absolutely firm about it.
MOOLCHAND: Shapoor. . .
SHAPOOR: Oh my God! My parents. My parents, what will happen to them?
CLARINDA: They won't be Shazia's burden now.
MOOLCHAND: Is there something I don't know.

Moolchand looks at Shapoor who drops his head.

CLARINDA: He hides things from you too? He put in an application to bring in his father and mother to Canada without telling his wife.
MOOLCHAND: In the family class? (*To Shapoor*) Why did you do that?
SHAPOOR: I can't say no to my father.
MOOLCHAND: I thought I told you . . .
CLARINDA: If you'll excuse me . . . (*She heads for the exit*)
SHAPOOR: Yes. But.
MOOLCHAND: Miss!. . Miss!!! . . . Please. . . . So what if he wants his parents with him. What's the problem?
CLARINDA: There's no problem. He'll have his parents with him—when he's back in Iran.
SHAPOOR: No, why would. . . .
MOOLCHAND: Okay, okay. He went about it in a wrong way. Let's punish him, but not destroy his life. . . .
CLARINDA: It's not my decision. Shazia has made up her mind.
SHAPOOR: She said this?
MOOLCHAND: She has or did someone. . . .
CLARINDA: (*To Shapoor*) That's why you shouldn't have hit her. Especially because you, your father and mother depend on her to come here. But you got her mad.
SHAPOOR: She got me madder.
CLARINDA: Then, you both are mad people.

Clarinda leaves.

PROUGAULT: Farhadi!
MOOLCHAND: Shapoor.
SHAPOOR: Shazia wouldn't say that.
MOOLCHAND: You are a certifiable idiot. Why in the family class? With that kind of money, they are investors before they are your family.
SHAPOOR: What?
MOOLCHAND: They should be put in "investor class". You fool. If you had listened to me, by now your father would have been buying up real estate in Laval. Now you can't transfer them to a different class.
SHAPOOR: Oh God, I am such an idiot, please, can't you do something?

Prougault steps forward.

PROUGAULT: Farhadi, let's go.
SHAPOOR: Mr. Moolchand.
MOOLCHAND: Wait Mr. President, I'll take responsibility over him. What forms must be signed? Who do I see? This boy needs to go home and clear his mind.
PROUGAULT: He will, as soon they can book a flight.
MOOLCHAND: What? What are you saying?
PROUGAULT : I've said enough, You're not his lawyer, let's go.
MOOLCHAND: Where are you taking him?
PROUGAULT: He will be in detention until deported home.
SHAPOOR: No!
MOOLCHAND: Hold on, deported?
SHAPOOR: No you can't do that!
PROUGAULT: Those are the immigration rules.
SHAPOOR: Please let me talk to Shazia.
MOOLCHAND: One more ethnic out of Canada eh Mr. President? what is going on here?
SHAPOOR: Where's Shazia?
MOOLCHAND: (*Turns to Shapoor*) Shapoor, let me handle this.
SHAPOOR: (*Loud*) Shazia! Shazia! I am sorry **Shazia**. . . .

Shapoor runs towards exit.

PROUGAULT: Officer!
SHAPOOR: . . . Please forgive me Shazia.

Amid loud shouting and screaming, Galliard enters pushing and shoving Shapoor back on the stage. Shapoor falls on the floor.

GALLIARD: Hey! Get back in the room.
MOOLCHAND: Shapoor, Shapoor. . . .
SHAPOOR: (*To Moolchand*) I only wanted to tell her . . .
MOOLCHAND: There, there, enough said. . . .
SHAPOOR: (*On the floor*) Please sir, I beg you, I am sorry. I promise I will never . . .
MOOLCHAND: Shapoor . . .
GALLIARD: Too late, you should have . . .
PROUGAULT: Galliard, shut up!
SHAPOOR: Please, you sir, Oh please, (*he cries*) I am sorry.
MOOLCHAND: Very well officers. Look at him, you have succeeded in scaring him. He will not strike his wife again. I assure you. Please, tell me what can we do?

Lights cross fade from them to Clarinda's office where Clarinda is talking to the family.

SHAZIA: Am I being cruel to him?
SHAFIQA: No, Shazia.
MURAD: Don't be ridiculous.
CLARINDA: You are being kind to yourself. I am very proud of you.
MURAD: Proud of a husbandless woman?
SHAFIQA: Murad!
CLARINDA: She has done something that no battered woman has.
SHAZIA: Clarinda, . . . I'm not doing this.
CLARINDA: This will send the message loud and clear. 'Cause back home he will have to explain why he was deported, . . . he'll have to face the embarrassment. Everybody will learn the price for hitting a woman. Here or anywhere.
MURAD: Well, good.
CLARINDA: Okay! We still have few legal things to do.
SHAZIA: I already signed the separation papers, didn't I?

CLARINDA: No, we need to discuss your share of the carpets.
SHAZIA: I don't want a cent from those
MURAD: You need the money.
SHAZIA: I don't want the carpets!
SHAFIQA: Shazia.
SHAZIA: No, Ma!
SHAFIQA: This girl is stupid. All she wants is to end her unhappy marriage as if marriage was ever a happy thing.
MURAD: As if she will become happy after ending her marriage.
SHAZIA: Abbu please!

Lights out on the family as we return to the present time. Courtroom spotlight appears on Prougault who has walked over to the door-frame by the family.

PROUGAULT: (*In spotlight*) Yes, I didn't know why he did it. He was always doing things like that. I had warned Sgt. Galliard about his behaviour many times. I am sorry, Guy. I tried to warn you. . . .

Flashback: lights come up on the police station. Galliard is working at the horizontally lying doorframe to act as a table. He stamps a report and gives it to Moolchand.

GALLIARD: No, no, he's not here, you can pick him up downstairs.
MOOLCHAND: That way? Thank you, you have been so kind. (*Sees Prougault*) Oh! hello Mr. President!
PROUGAULT: Has Farhadi been released?
GALLIARD: (*Surprised to see Prougault*) Oh! Did you hear this race tribunal guy?
PROUGAULT: Has Farhadi been released? Why did you just send Moolchand downstairs?
GALLIARD: Where does a guy like that get 10,000 dollars bond money from?
PROUGAULT: Sergeant. . . .
GALLIARD: Ethnic power.

Shapoor enters the scene.

SHAPOOR: Where is Mr. Moolchand?

Galliard steps towards Shapoor.

PROUGAULT: Guy, what are you doing?
GALLIARD: (*To Shapoor*) Listen, asshole, I can't keep you locked up, but if you go anywhere near her, I will ship you back to where you came from.
SHAPOOR: Ah, . . . ah . .
PROUGAULT: That's enough Galliard. O.K. Farhadi, go . . .

Shapoor starts to leave, Galliard grabs his arm and pulls him back.

(*Under his breath*) . . . Fuck.
GALLIARD: Listen boy, if you want to live in our country, you live by our rules. You understand that? You don't beat your women in this country! Bond or no bond you touched her and I will send you to hell.
PROUGAULT: (*To Shapoor*) Your friend is waiting downstairs. Ask for Lieut. Green. (*Shapoor exits*) Sergeant, you are too rough. What's the matter with you? Have you never heard of the term "libel suit"?

Lights fade out on them. We return to the present time. Lights come up on Clarinda's office. Rizvi family is present.

MURAD: No, I'd rather Shazia not be seen outside.
CLARINDA: Don't worry, he can't touch her any more.
SHAFIQA: No, no, it's because his friends will say, "there goes Rizvi's daughter who has brought shame to his family."
MURAD: Oh, be quiet.
SHAZIA: Abbu, ummi, I'll be okay. You can go back to Vancouver. Now, Naushad needs you more than I do. I'll be fine.
CLARINDA: Oh, your parents are leaving?
SHAZIA: Yes they were supposed to fly tomorrow to see my brother.
SHAFIQA: Yeah he needs us to babysit his brat so he can look after his video store. But we'll stay until. . .

Lights fade out on them. Courtroom spotlight appears on Moolchand, standing under the doorframe by the police station.

MOOLCHAND: (*In spotlight*) When I found out Shapoor died, I was not sure. He seemed to love his wife a great deal. But she seemed bent on destroying him. It was not good enough to divorce him. She wanted him deported, . . . gone, may be dead. I'm not saying she killed him. When he talked to me when I released him on bond. . . .

Flashback: as the lights change, we see Moolchand stepping out as though he was talking to an off-stage officer.

MOOLCHAND: (*To an off-stage officer*) Yes, tell him I'll be waiting outside.

Moolchand comes in front of the police station. Shapoor comes in from the police station.

SHAPOOR: Thank you very much for getting me out. Did you talk to Shazia?

MOOLCHAND: It's not over yet.

SHAPOOR: Did you tell her how sorry. . .

MOOLCHAND: You want your parents here, we have got to open a retail store and sell carpets.

SHAPOOR: Mr. Moolchand, how is she doing? I need to go home.

MOOLCHAND: Shapoor, Shapoor . . .

SHAPOOR: (*Moolchand hands him a paper*) What's this?

MOOLCHAND: Restraining order.

SHAPOOR: What? (*Pause*) Fuck! (*He starts to run*) I have to go.

MOOLCHAND: (*Grabs him*) You can't go. Listen, If you get closer than 100 yards to her, my friend, they will deport you.

SHAPOOR: Oh God, I look at my hands and I see my father's hands. I feel awful, I shouldn't have hit her.

MOOLCHAND: Yes, now do you want me to take care of the carpets?

SHAPOOR: I just want to tell her, I didn't mean it. I understand now why she didn't want my parents, . . . my father here. If she just gave me time I could have understood. I am not my father. Why? Why? I just kept hitting her hoping that she would see. I'm not my father.

MOOLCHAND: Is he that bad?

SHAPOOR: Sgt Galliard is right. Oh God, I need a policeman to protect my wife from me.

MOOLCHAND: Did he threaten you? Shapoor did he? What else did he tell you?

SHAPOOR: He is right. He's right . . .

MOOLCHAND: He's right about what?

SHAPOOR: May be I should be locked up.

MOOLCHAND: Do you know what that fucking cop did to you? Do you think the officer really cares for your wife? Look, my neighbour, a white guy, got drunk and made pulp out of his wife before passing out. The cop tells her, "Call us when he wakes up." Why didn't the cop arrest him?

SHAPOOR: (*In Persian*) Behmensha.

MOOLCHAND: That cop had nothing to gain by arresting one of his own tribesman. It is only when they find someone "different" they get all dutiful. And then they get your wife to collaborate with them.

SHAPOOR: If I could talk to her . . .

MOOLCHAND: Go home, break the restraining order, see what they do.

SHAPOOR: But Mr Moolchand, maybe she won't . . .

MOOLCHAND: She is kicking you out of the country.

SHAPOOR: She can't, you have a bond on me.

MOOLCHAND: The bond can't protect you from being deported.

SHAPOOR: What?

MOOLCHAND: Where do you think the bond money came from anyway? (*Pause*) Your carpets.

SHAPOOR: All the carpets?

MOOLCHAND: Yes.

SHAPOOR: My father . . .

MOOLCHAND: Just until this is all settled. That's why we need to open a store and sell those carpets, but to do that I have to keep you in the country? We have to find a way to stop them from making an example of you.

SHAPOOR: What the fuck are you talking about?
MOOLCHAND: Have you ever heard of anyone getting kicked out of the city, let alone the country for hitting their wife? They're using you to scare us.
SHAPOOR: Why are they doing this to me?

In the following lines, Moolchand speaks with a Canadian accent instead of his usual East Indian.

MOOLCHAND: I don't know. Because you are a muslim. And they think you are all terrorists, out to get Salman Rushdie, blow up the Bay street, your people breed like crazy . . . might take over Canada. Don't you get it? Your community is a growing concern to them, . . . taking over entire suburbs, shopping malls, I don't know. Your community is doing pretty good for a minority, but hey, then you utter the word minority, everybody thinks about blacks only.
SHAPOOR: Mr. Moolchand, what happened to your accent?

Lights fade out on Shapoor. A rapid transition to courtroom spotlight appearing on Moolchand.

MOOLCHAND: (*In spotlight, regaining his accent*) Against the police, Immigration and the justice system. Shapoor's only fault is that he struck his wife. But that didn't even leave a mark on her body. But then he was also begging her for her mercy, . . . and yes, Shapoor was about to set up a business, may have created a couple of jobs. What does he get in punishment? *Deportation!* I say that the system didn't work. This boy did not die in vain and I plan to do something about it. They will see what this minority can do!

Lights out on Moolchand. Courtroom spotlight appears on Clarinda who is standing at a spot near her office.

CLARINDA: (*In the spotlight*) No! No! No! He did not care about anyone your Honour, Shapoor or Shazia. He doesn't know what it's like to be hit. 'Cause he does all the hitting. If I were you, check where those carpets are now. Who is selling them?

Flashback: lights come up on Clarinda's office. She moves out of the courtroom spot to her office. Looks for some files as Moolchand walks in.

MOOLCHAND: No, no, please. First give me an opportunity to greet you.

CLARINDA: Alright.

MOOLCHAND: How are you?

CLARINDA: How about you?

MOOLCHAND: Clarinda, I need your help, I really do.

CLARINDA: How?

MOOLCHAND: It's about Shapoor . . .

CLARINDA: I'm sorry Mr. Moolchand I . . .

MOOLCHAND: I know how you feel. Please listen, he's a good man with so much potential. I know right now that he can't control his rage, but he needs our help. He can't get help if he is thrown out. What I am saying is—us, the East Indians, the Africans,the Chinese . . . you know—people like you and me. If we are to survive, we must be united. Help each other.

CLARINDA: Because we are coloureds?

MOOLCHAND: Without Shazia, Shapoor has nobody here, no family no support, nothing. Right now he happens to be one of the many unfortunate men in this country because he happens to be the man of wrong colour and culture.

CLARINDA: Nobody's culture equals torture. He hit her because he is a man and she is a woman. It's nothing to do with culture.

MOOLCHAND: Please, listen to me—listen to me, . . . help us. He is not a typical Canuck, opens a beer, watches hockey and scores punches at the wife for fun.

CLARINDA: No, he doesn't play hockey.

MOOLCHAND: He's one of us, see?

CLARINDA: Isn't *she* also one of us?

MOOLCHAND: That's why she shouldn't deport him.

CLARINDA: And give him an opportunity to attack her again. And turn the crime against her into her own fault, no!

MOOLCHAND: (*Pulls out a declaration*) O.K. This thing bears the signatures of some very important ethnic leaders, including a couple of ethnic MPs.

CLARINDA: (*Glancing*) Signatures for what?

MOOLCHAND: Stop his deportation.

CLARINDA: Where did you get all these?

MOOLCHAND: I'm trying to help Shapoor.

CLARINDA: I'm trying to protect Shazia.

MOOLCHAND: Somebody should try to forgive him.

CLARINDA: Somebody is trying to forget him.

MOOLCHAND: Is that why she has gone public?

CLARINDA: (*Sarcastic*) God forbid, the victims go public and the world might hear them.

MOOLCHAND: But what do we hear—victims? No. Miss Clarinda Keith's "zero tolerance" in the Gazette. Shapoor's father is a lunatic on the CBC. How about hearing him? No wonder she provokes the hell out of him.

CLARINDA: Provoking ain't a crime, battering is. Got that?

MOOLCHAND: Got it.

CLARINDA: Excuse me, I'm busy. (*She gets up*)

MOOLCHAND: You know, you're a very determined woman . . . you'll need to be. (*Brings out another letter*) Some of us want an inquiry.

CLARINDA: I know.

MOOLCHAND: Look again. (*Gives her the letter*) Inquiry into a larger problem, Inquiry into what Sgt Galliard did?

CLARINDA: What?

MOOLCHAND: Galliard is a racist.

CLARINDA: A woman was assaulted here.

MOOLCHAND: He racially assaulted Shapoor.

CLARINDA: You can't be serious. That's not the issue here.

MOOLCHAND: Right here in Montreal, eight coloured men have been shot dead by the officers and you want to tell me the officers aren't racist.

CLARINDA: Galliard isn't one of them.

MOOLCHAND: Just the other day the officers looked very happy, because there was a black taxi-driver in custody. When the officers have that smile on their faces, and there is a black man in custody, do you know what's coming?

CLARINDA: Don't teach me what racism is!

MOOLCHAND: Just because you are a shade darker?

CLARINDA: Get the hell out of my office.

MOOLCHAND: Guy Galliard is a chronic racist.

CLARINDA: He saved that woman's life.

MOOLCHAND: I want him removed from his job.

CLARINDA: What kind of man are you? Do you know what you're trying to do here? There is no other officer who runs the domestic unit as well as Galliard does. You take him to the inquiry and I'll be his expert witness. Now get out.

MOOLCHAND: Bravo! Bravo. A black, turned activist, turned expert, turned witness to a racist cop! I hate to say it, but there is something wrong with a person who doesn't stand by her own community.

CLARINDA: Shazia's my community.

MOOLCHAND: Every time you open your mouth, whoop, a cliche spills out of it.

CLARINDA: Out!

MOOLCHAND: Let's both take a deep breath.

CLARINDA: Out!

MOOLCHAND: Don't you think the whites hate us enough already? Do you want to give them one more excuse to hate us?

CLARINDA: Whites don't have time to hate us. They are too busy paying the bills and raising their families.

MOOLCHAND: And you're too busy chasing a poor ethnic out of the country.

CLARINDA: Cut the crap, Canada deports drug dealers, not a wife beater.

MOOLCHAND: Then it's sad you are doing this country's dirty work. (*Flashing the paper*) Well it's my turn to talk to the press. People in the community must know where you stand.

CLARINDA: Get out or I'll call the police.

MOOLCHAND: The police? That confirms where you stand. I am going but I want you to think about something. There is an immigrant business in the making. There is a troubled young man, there is his sick father. I just want you to remember this.

Lights fade out on them. We return to the present time. Murad can be seen standing outside the family home, in dim lights. Courtroom spotlight appears on Shafiqa who is standing near the doorframe by her house.

SHAFIQA: (*In spotlight*) No, no your Honour. My husband—he was so possessed—shame—he said—our lives were filled with shame. I don't know why he says these things. He is a gentle man your honour. He could not have done that. He could not have killed that poor boy, But your Honour, he was just so upset with our community.

Flashback: as the spotlights go out on her, she exits. Lights come up on the house. Murad enters in a bad irritated mood. He is coming from the mosque. Puts down his coat.

MURAD: (*Calling*) Shafiqa, . . . Shafiqa.
SHAFIQA: (*Off-stage*) In the kitchen.
MURAD: Come out.
SHAFIQA: You worried what goes on in your wife's kitchen?

Shafiqa enters.

MURAD: Accidents and I eat them. Do you know what are they saying in the meeting? Mr. Moolchand. . . .
SHAFIQA: Don't make it harder for her.
MURAD: Why can't she behave the way daughters behave back home?
MURAD: Shazia! Shazia!
SHAFIQA: She is with Clarinda.
MURAD: The black woman.
SHAFIQA: Yes, to register something.
MURAD: Is Clarinda married?
SHAFIQA: No, she is happy.
MURAD: How can a woman who makes her living breaking families, be happy? I'll not allow her in this house.
SHAFIQA: That's enough, take off your shoes—come and eat.
MURAD: You know, nobody talked to me at the mosque. They all

think that failure of the daughter is due to failure of the father. Shazia has no shame in being husbandless, but I do.

SHAFIQA: I didn't know you wanted a husband.

MURAD: It's not a joke. I have to take Shazia to the Imam.

SHAFIQA: No Mullah is going to decide my daughter's fate.

MURAD: You don't live in the real world, do you? What will happen to her? What man will marry her?

SHAFIQA: One who won't hit her, now come and eat.

MURAD. (*Showing her a newspaper*) No wait, look what they say about her. Look! Do you have any idea who marries a divorced woman? A convict, a handicap or an old widower with ten children. Is that what you want for her? Shafiqa Begum, nobody wants a divorced woman, she is all used up, . . . nothing left, not even her dignity.

SHAFIQA: (*With deep hurt*) Used up? It's our daughter you're talking about. Shame on you. I am ashamed of you.

MURAD: Remember when it happened between my sister and her husband? Didn't my father go to the mullah?

SHAFIQA: (*Ridiculing*) And that stupid Mullah said, (*Mocking*) "lock her, starve her, give her a chance to behave before you can smack her."

MURAD: You say what you please, but the next day, he bought her an expensive saree and she was fine.

SHAFIQA: No wonder she had so many expensive sarees.

MURAD: That's not the point!

SHAFIQA: My daughter will not go to any Mullah.

MURAD: Alright then, let's move out of the city, where there is no Mullah and no Clarinda.

SHAFIQA: And no Moolchand!

MURAD: Do you know what Moolchand said at the meeting? "We don't need the RCMP to kick out an ethnic. We need a Canadian wife to do that."

SHAFIQA: When you go to the next meeting, tell that mullah and Moolchand, if they say a word about my daughter, I will chase *them* out of the country now come and eat!

As lights go out on the family, we come to the present time. Courtroom spotlight appears on Galliard who is standing under the door-

frame by Clarinda's office.

GALLIARD: (*In spotlight*) I remember when my dad got mad, my mom got beat up. He kicked the door, ripped the phone, threw food and pulled big handfuls of her hair. My dad was 6 feet, 300 pounds. When he got started, my brother ran to pull the curtains and I hid behind the door with my hands to my ears and my eyes closed. My mother died and everybody believed it was in her sleep. (*Pause*) So when I see someone beat his woman, part of me says, send him to hell. Is that racist, judge?

Flashback: lights come up on Prougault who is standing downstage centre. The doorframe has been lowered horizontally to act as a platform/table. Galliard walks over to him.

PROUGAULT: He's charged you with racial misconduct.
GALLIARD: Bullshit.

Prougault gives him a letter.

PROUGAULT: I have tried to warn you, Guy.
GALLIARD: (*Blows a "phew", reads*) *"Cultural Insensitivity or Racism: "Police still white"*. So?
PROUGAULT: Every word that scares the hell out of a white cop, is here . . . used excessive force and racial slurs. . . .
GALLIARD: Come on officer, do you know one cop who doesn't use foul language?
PROUGAULT: Not foul language, Sergeant, racial language.
GALLIARD: The other day I called a Scotsman a skirt-wearing dyke and he called me a "French toad."
PROUGAULT: (*Looking at the paper*) You called him an Iranian.
GALLIARD: So?
PROUGAULT: You denied him his "Canadian identity".
GALLIARD: And if I called him Canadian, wouldn't I be denying him his "ethnic roots." I don't chase words, I chase criminals.
PROUGAULT: You're famous! Sarge, haven't you seen the paper today? You're on the front page, you're on the front page of every newspaper. And on Chief's desk. When you go home to-

night, tell your wife and son, "I'm racist." An Iranian made you famous, Guy.

GALLIARD: I'd' like to break that Currichand's neck.

PROUGAULT: Shut up Sergeant. I don't need your garbage mouth doing any more damage. Every ethnic leader and bleeding heart white is calling! Fuck, I don't need another inquiry, not with the union election coming up.

GALLIARD; What inquiry?

PROUGAULT: The chief has ordered an inquiry.

GALLIARD: He thinks I am a racist?

PROUGAULT: He got a call from Bouchard's office. Damage control after Parizeau's ethnic remark.

GALLIARD: Bouchard?

PROUGAULT: You're the first victim Guy. ". . .We lost the referendum because of the ethnics." The man lost the battle of his life because he didn't have ethnics on his side. Surly Mr. Bouchard has to woo ethnics. How do you expect the chief not to call an inquiry?

GALLIARD: Bullshit!

PROUGAULT: He ain't got the race card up his sleeves. "Will that be cash or credit? Put it on my race card baby." You can charge "justice" to the race card. Used to be blacks. Now, it's every fucking shade of people. Racism has turned into a contagious disease.

GALLIARD: An inquiry, because of this Iranian bastard, Jesus . . .

PROUGAULT: (*Flashing a document*) Moolchand doesn't know when to stop. Now he's saying, "we should have ethnics serving ethnic criminals."

GALLIARD: Really!! When an ethnic smacks his wife, we must find a cop of matching colour and race. May be it'd better if I just killed the guy instead of calling him an Iranian.

PROUGAULT: Sergeant, shut up.

GALLIARD: I ain't a racist. Clarinda knows that and she's black. She and I have worked together plenty of times.

PROUGAULT: Guy, Clarinda is fixated on gender—she wants more ladies in the force because ladies serve ladies better.

GALLIARD: That's great. I will teach my boy—you want something—Just blame someone. Women blame men, blacks blame whites, homos blame heteros. (*Laughs*) But that's fine because I'll do my job.

PROUGAULT: Sarge you are being removed from the domestic unit until the inquiry clears you.

GALLIARD: What the fuck?

PROUGAULT: I warned you.

GALLIARD: That ain't fair.

PROUGAULT: I'm sorry.

GALLIARD: Ten years of service, hundreds of citations . . .

PROUGAULT: I have no choice. Moolchand got his wish.

As lights go out on them, Galliard walks back to the doorframe. We come back to the present time. Courtroom spotlight appears on Galliard.

GALLIARD: (*In the spotlight*) I was trained to run the domestic unit. That's my job! And I had to sit around some desk while he ran around. And what if he hit her again? No-one would care.

Lights fade out on Galliard. Courtroom spotlight appears on Murad who is on the other side of the stage, standing under the doorframe by his house.

MURAD: (*In spotlight*) Your honour, if you would have seen Shazia, before she married this . . . this man, . . . We had such hopes for her. Our little chatterbox. We called her that. 'Cause she talked and talked until her jaws began to hurt of talking and she would fall asleep. We were always . . .

Flashback: lights come up on the house. We see Shazia sleeping in her bed. Murad steps out of the doorframe and enters his house.

SHAFIQA: Shh. Don't scream. (*Looks at Shazia*) Poor girl, came back from the doctor and hasn't said a word.

MURAD: (*Kisses Shazia's forehead*) Shafiqa begum, I never imagined that I would ever smell beer in my daughter's breath. Baap rey baap.

Lights out on the family.

Note: From here to end of Moolchand's speech, lights will shift from one actor to the other in quick succession as they talk to create a semblance that things are happening simultaneously.

Light come up on Moolchand who is delivering a speech.

MOOLCHAND: Yes I want coloureds on the force, but not by preferential treatment. I say that if you have 10 dollars, you must get the same value for your ten dollars whether you are white or black. Do the non-whites have the same opportunity as their white brothers, to earn those ten dollars? That is not me talking. No. That is the Auditor General of Canada, . . . and yes, he is not a whining Mr. Moolchand, he is a white man who has the courage to say the truth.

Lights shift from Moolchand to Shazia who has woken up, unnoticed. Murad pulls out a letter.

SHAFIQA: What's that?

MURAD: (*Whispers*) Major sahib is still shopping for a bride abroad for his son.

SHAFIQA: What will you do when Major sahib finds out that your daughter is all "used up"?

MURAD: He is our best bet.

Shazia gets up.

SHAZIA: Are you betting on me?

MURAD: No, no beti, I'm not betting on you, but you need a husband.

SHAZIA: I don't need a husband, I have a husband.

MURAD: If I talked to my father like that, aray baap rey baap.

SHAZIA: Aray baap rey what? Why must you find a husband for me? Because I am a misfit, I drink sometimes? I want divorce and a muslim woman is not allowed to. Is that your baap rey what? Abbu, why must I defend myself?

Shazia breaks into tears, exits.

MURAD: Shazia. . . .
SHAFIQA: Beti. . . .

Light shifts from the family to Moolchand, who continues with his speech.

MOOLCHAND: I think violence towards women is appalling. From the culture I come from, women are treated with respect.

Light shifts from Moolchand to the family . . .

SHAFIQA: Are you happy now?
MURAD: Would you be happy if your daughter scolded you?
SHAFIQA: Murad we have to help her.
MURAD: I just wanted to find her a new husband so she won't have to . . . to live in the fear of the old one.
SHAFIQA: Really?
MURAD: Yes really? What do you think?

Shazia enters.

SHAZIA: Abbu, Ummi, You don't have to stay for me. Just go to Vancouver now.

Shazia exits. Light shifts from the family to Galliard who is standing under the doorframe by Clarinda's office.

GALLIARD: I'm not guilty! I swore to tell the truth and . . .

Light shifts from Galliard to the family . . .

MURAD: Does she really want us to leave?
SHAFIQA: Of course not. She is just upset with you. Come, let's go for a walk. Let her clear her mind. Then I'll talk to her. (*Calling*) Beti, lock the door, we will be back soon.
SHAZIA: (*Off-stage*) Okay.

Murad and Shafiqa exit as the light shift from the family to Mool-

chand. . . . Meanwhile Shapoor walks over to the house. He stands outside in dim light.

MOOLCHAND: That's why I want coloureds in the force, to work side by side with the white cops. So that the white cop will see that the coloured cop next to him is just as human as anybody else. The best way to win your enemy is to love your enemy.

Lights shift from Moolchand to the family, where Shazia is alone. She hears a knock.

SHAZIA: Who is it? Didn't you take the key, ma?

She opens the door and finds Shapoor at her door. Shazia steps back.

SHAPOOR: Don't. Please. Don't call the police. Please.
SHAZIA: You shouldn't be here.
SHAPOOR: I just want to talk.
SHAZIA: What?
SHAPOOR: (*Pause*) Hi . . .
SHAZIA: Hi . . .
SHAPOOR: I thought may be you moved.
SHAZIA: Well I didn't.

Lights shift from the family home to the women's shelter. Clarinda and Galliard talking . . .

GALLIARD: Well at first I just told him not to move.
CLARINDA: Did he?
GALLIARD: Well no, but it was all very fast. I mean I didn't know how badly she was hurt.
CLARINDA: Did Shapoor try to run?

Lights shift from the shelter to the family.

SHAPOOR: I called, but you've taken an unlisted number.
SHAZIA: You better go now. My parents will be . . .
SHAPOOR: Please Shazia, don't hate me. I have nobody to turn to.

My family . . . they're in danger. (*Pause*) I would not risk coming here if it wasn't serious. (*Pause*) Please . . . I'm begging. Just listen to me and I'll go. (*Steps towards Shazia, she moves back*) I won't move. (*She stops*) (*Pause*) Please don't be afraid of me.

Shapoor takes a step towards her.

SHAZIA: Don't move. Please.
SHAPOOR: Shazia, How are you?
SHAZIA: What do you want?
SHAPOOR: Shazia.
SHAZIA: Shapoor.
SHAPOOR: My mother and father. . . . Please, let me finish. They're in danger, they had to flee from Iran.
SHAZIA: Where to? Mirabel without a visa?
SHAPOOR: They escaped to India. They are in a jail, in Bombay.
SHAZIA: What kind of business is your father doing?
SHAPOOR: The Iranian government put him on the list to be tried.

Lights shift from the family to Prougault who is sitting on a stool at an angle from the audiences, at the front of the stage .

PROUGAULT: I understand where this Moolchand is coming from. (*Pause*) Once I went to Toronto . . . on a private visit. I took the bus, the driver was an Indian. Not Indian Indian, East Indian? In Toronto a lot of them are driving buses. He told me that I was a dime short but I was sure that I had put the right fare. So I dropped another dime. And throughout the ride, that's all that I thought about, . . . a coloured guy telling me I was a dime short.

Lights shift from Prougault to the family.

SHAZIA: Because you, fool of a son, you put them in the family class.
SHAPOOR: He is locked in a jail full of criminals. Shazia, you know my father is very ill. This shock may kill him.
SHAZIA: What do you want? Money?
SHAPOOR: No, the only way I can bring them to safety is if . . . if

you, . . . if I 'm not deported.

Lights shift from the family to Moolchand who continues with his speech.

MOOLCHAND: Let's not forget, Shapoor did something wrong, a horrible act that unfortunately so many men do. I don't condone him. But I wish we lived in a society where we learn to understand why the problem exists, heal it, hate the wrong, not the wrongdoer. That is why I will not allow . . .

Light shift from Moolchand to Shazia and Shapoor again.

SHAZIA: I can't. . . .

SHAPOOR: I am begging you to just delay the divorce . . . so that . . .

SHAZIA: Delay? You do want a divorce?

SHAPOOR: Only until you . . .

SHAZIA: What am I? A bargaining chip to negotiate your father's escape?

SHAPOOR: No, I love you.

Lights shift from the family home to Clarinda's office.

GALLIARD: A i i r a n . . .Yeah I said that because I knew that he would listen, you know get his attention.

CLARINDA: Why, what was he doing?

GALLIARD: He was very, . . . you know, . . . moving around . . . quick, jerky . . . agitated—kind of . . . you know?

Lights shift from Clarinda's office to Shazia and Shapoor at home.

SHAZIA: Why is that policeman under *inquiry*? Who made them investigate Clarinda's ethics—I can't even see her again, until this inquiry is over.

SHAPOOR: I know, I know, I don't know what to do about Moolchand, he's out of control.

SHAZIA: I'm a bar-hopping slut who has no respect for family values.

SHAPOOR: No, I'll tell him to stop. I promise.
SHAZIA: When? When I am dragged into court?
SHAPOOR: I promise I will break all ties with Moolchand, alright?
SHAZIA: Provided I delay the divorce until your father arrives safely in Canada.
SHAPOOR: Yes, no, please.
SHAZIA: Get out.

Lights shift from Shazia and Shapoor to Clarinda's office again.

CLARINDA: That's all you said? Guy, this inquiry's not a joke. It's important you remember everything a little clearer.
GALLIARD: I didn't stop to memorize everything I did. Every situation is different. When you walk in there, . . . it's not easy you know, you never know if he is waiting behind some door, has a gun, . . . you know?

Lights shift back to Shazia and Shapoor.

SHAZIA: No. (*Shapoor stands still*) Leave or I call . . . the police.
SHAPOOR: Don't, I was wrong, I didn't know any better.
SHAZIA: And you never will! Leave.

Lights shift from them to Prougault . . .

PROUGAULT: I mean, this guy remembers his fucking history. Two centuries under the English. Now he thinks it is his turn to get back. A kind of show of power.
GALLIARD: (*Turning in Prougault's direction*) Getting back at the English, eh?
PROUGAULT: Do I look English to you?
GALLIARD: You act very French.
PROUGAULT: (*Pause*) Yeah . . .

Lights shift to the home. In a sudden outburst of anger, Shapoor rushes and grabs Shazia.

SHAZIA: Let me go! You'll be sorry if you don't . . .

SHAPOOR: I am sorry, I said I am sorry, . . . But you won't listen I am sorry. . . . Listen to me, . . . I am sorry, . . . my whole God damned life is sorry. . .
SHAZIA: You're hurting me!

Shapoor throws her down on the bed. Shazia screams as the lights shift from them to Moolchand.

MOOLCHAND: Some of my best friends are white. Just the other day a white woman told me she would have married me instead of her fourth husband.

Lights shift from Moolchand to the family again.

SHAPOOR: No. You be sorry too. Call the newspaper, what's the number? (*Picks up the phone*) Call them, tell them, ... (*He picks up the phone book, starts to rip pages, looking for a number, repeats his words*) I am sorry . . . say sorry. . . .
SHAZIA: Go away!
SHAPOOR: Not before telling everyone.

He rips pages from the telephone book. Crushes the pages in his fist and repeatedly throws them at Shazia. Shazia covering her head, falls down on the floor. Shapoor stands over her and stuffs torn pages in her mouth in uncontrollable rage. . . .

. . . . You are going to call the newspaper and tell them. I want the world to know that my father is dying and you don't give a fuck. (*He dials*) Say you are sorry, . . . you'll—Hello, yes, . . . who writes the front page? What, . . . what, . . . No! . . Wait . . . (*He hands the phone to Shazia*) Say sorry, . . . sorry . . . sorry. . . .

Then Shapoor stops, . . . steps back. Shazia lifts her body from the floor, and falls back. We hear her cries. . . . Shapoor drops the phone and starts to cry in shame. Lights shift from them to Moolchand, who continues with his speech.

MOOLCHAND: My friends, let the truth be spoken: A police force which sees a criminal in a person of colour, is incapable of treating us as human beings.

Lights shift from Moolchand to Shazia's house again. Shafiqa and Murad return. See Shazia . . .

SHAFIQA: Oh, my God . . .
MURAD: Hi, Allah . . .

Lights shifts from the family to Prougault.

PROUGAULT: And then, when I was getting off the bus, I saw my dime on the floor. I held it up to him. "Here it is," but he didn't even look. I waved "take care man." He says, "You too."
GALLIARD: (*Turning in Prougault's direction, ridiculing*) He said, "you too," eh?
PROUGAULT: So I understand what Moolchand wants to be and what he is. He is not black, he is not white. He's a mongrel.

Lights shift from Prougault to the family. Shafiqa takes Shazia away. Shapoor walks across the stage miming as if he was being taken away, handcuffed. Lights fade out on the family.
General lights come up on Prougault who is talking to Clarinda. Meanwhile Murad is seen picking up torn pages from the floor of his house in dim lights.

PROUGAULT: Every cop was tried.
CLARINDA: When was the last cop punished?
PROUGAULT: Have you heard the term "benefit of the doubt"?
CLARINDA: What doubt? Killing's a crime even if it is done by a cop. That's why Moolchand has become your headache. He is not Galliard's problem, the brotherhood is. Do yourself a favour, if you get reelected, clean up the brotherhood.
PROUGAULT: You know what's funny? Ethnics don't act mistreated unless they are caught breaking the law.
GALLIARD: (*Off-stage*) Fuck!
CLARINDA: What?
PROUGAULT: What happened?

Galliard enters.

GALLIARD: Restraining order, eh? That Iranian attacked his wife again.
CLARINDA: Oh my God, Shazia. . . .
GALLIARD: (*To Clarinda*) Queen Elizabeth hospital.
CLARINDA: Thank you, . . . Oh god.

Clarinda rushes off.

PROUGAULT: (*Calling*) Should I send one of my men to arrest him or look for an Iranian cop?
GALLIARD: They just picked him up. He's down the hall. . . .

Galliard starts to go in that direction.

PROUGAULT: Galliard! Get back to your desk. The two of you have done enough damage around here already.

Lights fade out on them. Courtroom spotlight appears on Murad who is standing under the doorframe by his house.

MURAD: (*In spotlight*) Has your daughter ever been beaten to the last thread of her life? (*Pause*) I'm sorry, yes I am sorry your honour, . . . It's just when you hold your little daughter in your arms and you realize she needs you, . . . my help. I . . .

Courtroom spotlight fades out on Murad. Lights come up on the detention cell. Shapoor is sitting on a stool, devastated, distraught and incoherent. Moolchand enters through the doorframe. Meanwhile Prougault stands outside the cell.

SHAPOOR: Mr. Moolchand. . . .
MOOLCHAND: Iranian shithead. Complete shithead. Why don't you take on someone your own size? Idiot. What will I tell everybody now? That I'm protecting a proven wife-beater?
SHAPOOR: Forgive me please.
MOOLCHAND: Shut up. We were getting somewhere. We were fi-

nally going to have some coloured cops on the force. You were going to give the most important testimony. You blew it. I had Galliard cornered, I could have proven him a racist.

SHAPOOR: You won't have to prove anything any more. I'm withdrawing the charges against Galliard.

MOOLCHAND: What?

Moolchand hits Shapoor with the newspaper, several times. Shapoor covers and goes down on the floor.

MOOLCHAND: Gaddha! That is a slap in my face . . . a big bloody slap.

SHAPOOR: Please I won't ask anything more. Just get me out of here. I won't go near her, I won't .

MOOLCHAND: I can't. Not this time.

SHAPOOR: I don't want any more courts, any more Galliards . . .

MOOLCHAND: The moment you withdraw the charges, they will throw you out of the country.

SHAPOOR: I want to be thrown out of the country. Do it for me.

Moolchand slaps Shapoor.

MOOLCHAND: (*Pause*) I am sorry. How do you think you can get your mother and father out of Tihar jail in India? You want them alive, you have to stay in Canada.

SHAPOOR: (*Tearful*) I can't fight with my wife any more. I just can't.

MOOLCHAND: Alright, alright.

SHAPOOR: I want to leave this country, please.

MOOLCHAND: Quiet! Let me think.

SHAPOOR: I can't live like this any more.

MOOLCHAND: Calm down, . . . please.

SHAPOOR: (*Whispers*) Please, help me. . . . Please get me out of here. I promise I will not come back. Sell all those carpets if you . . .

PROUGAULT: (*Off-stage*) Time is up.

MOOLCHAND: Shh. . . . Shut up—shut up. Don't speak with any one until I come back.

Shapoor, like a helpless child, grabs Moolchand with both his arms .

SHAPOOR: (*Hugging Moolchand's knees*) Don't go, . . . No, . . . Please.

MOOLCHAND: I will be back soon .

Moolchand stands him up, hugs him, and whispers something secretly in his ears. Prougault, who was standing outside, in dim lights, steps under the doorframe.

PROUGAULT: Time up mister.

MOOLCHAND: Come on stand up. Yes, Thank you, thank you sir.

Moolchand exits. Prougault, resting against the doorframe, whistles to draw Shapoor's attention.

PROUGAULT: (*To Shapoor*) If 100 thousand French Canadian landed in India, what do you think would happen? . . . They'd screw up the country?

SHAPOOR: I don't know.

PROUGAULT: Here we have 100 thousand Moolchands in Quebec. And what do you think they are doing?

SHAPOOR: I 'm sorry sir, I don't know!

PROUGAULT: I think you do. Get up.

Shapoor extends his arms to be handcuffed.

No, I'm not putting any handcuffs on you. No (*Pointing*) . . . that door.

Lights fade out on Shapoor and Prougault. Courtroom spotlights alternate in quick succession on Clarinda and Moolchand.
Courtroom spotlight on Clarinda.

CLARINDA: (*In spotlight*) It hurts, it wasn't fair.

Courtroom spotlight on Moolchand.

MOOLCHAND: (*In spotlight*) When the inquiry was postponed, I was afraid another racist cop would not be punished.

Courtroom spotlight on Clarinda.

CLARINDA: (*In spotlight*) It didn't seem to hurt Mr. Prougault's union campaign or Moolchand's quest for more coloureds on the force.

Courtroom spotlight on Moolchand.

MOOLCHAND: (*In spotlight*) With Shapoor's disappearance, I had to dig up many more witnesses against Galliard.

Courtroom spotlight on Clarinda.

CLARINDA: (*In spotlight*) The police knew it, the judges knew it, but, they let him slip away. Why bother? She's just a woman.

Courtroom spotlight out on both of them. General lights come up. They cross each other's path as they walk out of their respective courtroom spots.

MOOLCHAND: Miss Clarinda, we will see each other in two weeks?

CLARINDA: I don't have time for this bullshit. Why didn't Shapoor turn-up today for the inquiry?

MOOLCHAND: I don't know.

CLARINDA: What? You stalling for time?

MOOLCHAND: O.K., If you really want to know, I just found out, he fled the country.

CLARINDA: WHAT ???

MOOLCHAND: I went to put a bail on him (*Pulls out the bail*) . . . but Prougault told me that Shapoor was freed on a stricter restraining order.

CLARINDA: Prougault? How come you didn't mention it in there?

MOOLCHAND: I just got the call from Heathrow Airport London. The boy called to say that he was en-route to India.

CLARINDA: Does he know, if he flees the country with a criminal charge, he'll never be allowed back.

MOOLCHAND: That is why I did not believe him on the phone.

CLARINDA: Where are you hiding him.

MOOLCHAND: Why should I hide him?

CLARINDA: Because you're afraid to lose and you didn't want him to face the judge today.

MOOLCHAND: Miss Keith, please learn to trust someone.

CLARINDA: Trust? Did he trust you with his carpets?

MOOLCHAND: Look I want this inquiry over just as much as you, —so we can finally settle this issue. . . .

CLARINDA: There's a young woman lying in the hospital.

MOOLCHAND: Then you should be happy, her attacker, isn't around. I'm almost happy he left. How do you think it makes me look defending a wife beater? You wanted him deported, he's gone.

CLARINDA: You're a wretched piece of scum.

MOOLCHAND: There is no need for name calling. Good bye. Oh Ms Clarinda, there's one thing. Now that he's out of the country and can't harm the girl, could you convince her to drop the charge against the boy so I can get my bond money!

CLARINDA: As if nothing ever happened?

MOOLCHAND: The inquiry was just postponed, that will happen.

CLARINDA: (*Bitterly sarcastic*) Without the man who was "assaulted." Without your star witness?

Clarinda exits, Moolchand rushes after her.

MOOLCHAND: (*Shouts*) He is gone away, not the racism.

Lights come up on the family. Shazia is seated between her parents. Everybody is in sombre mood.

MURAD: Oh my God, oh my God, please help me.

SHAFIQA: Why didn't you tell me?

SHAZIA: I didn't know.

SHAFIQA: You're four months pregnant and you didn't know?

MURAD: Four months?

SHAFIQA: What planet do you live on?

SHAZIA: At first the doctor thought it was stress. I didn't know.

MURAD: Stress!

SHAFIQA: You'll know the meaning of stress when you are a mother.

SHAZIA: (*Facing her mother*) I'm going to keep the baby.

Murad gets up angrily . . .

MURAD: Now she wants to be a good muslim?

SHAFIQA: Are you insane girl?

SHAZIA: I want the baby.

MURAD: What will people say?

SHAZIA: I don't care.

MURAD: Who will marry you now?

SHAZIA: Abbu, please!!

MURAD: Don't please me, . . . please. No decent man will marry you.

SHAZIA: I'm still married.

MURAD: And I'll take care of that.

Murad walks away. Lights begin to dim on Shazia as she talks.

SHAZIA: How? How? How with him, . . . so far away. God knows where, . . . I can't believe he would do this. Just leave. So spineless. . . . No care for me. Just . . . just, . . . nothing. This is all I have.

Murad walks back to Shazia, holds her . . .

MURAD: No, . . what have I said? Ah little chatterbox. My little . . .

Shazia cries in her father's arms.

SHAFIQA: Murad, you go in the other room.

Murad leaves.

SHAZIA: Ma, I want the baby.

SHAFIQA: What if the baby grows up to be like his father?
SHAZIA: I can't know that.
SHAFIQA: I am afraid Shazia. With this baby, you are inviting the man back into your life.
SHAZIA: I don't want him, I want the baby.

Lights fade out on the family. Courtroom spotlight appears on Prougault . . .

PROUGAULT: (*In spotlight*) I mean it all seemed very suspicious how Farhadi disappeared right before the inquiry. We checked everywhere. We thought Mr. Moolchand was hiding him. We checked the airlines, and found he left the country. But it didn't matter, we had an inquiry didn't we? (*Listens*) What? Yes I was responsible. . . . No, No we couldn't keep him in the station any longer. What purpose would it have served?

Flashback: spotlight out on Prougault. Lights come up centre-stage. Prougault steps in. Galliard, who has just come out of the inquiry, joins him. He is aggravated.

GALLIARD: That was a fucking circus, not an inquiry.
PROUGAULT: Sarge, listen to me.
GALLIARD: God damn . . . makes me sick. I want to get the hell out of here.
PROUGAULT: Wait, wait a minute sarge.
GALLIARD: Don't call me that. I'm not a goddamned Sergeant any more. They wouldn't even let me talk.
PROUGAULT: Inquiries are arbitration, not judgements.
GALLIARD: What am I going to do now? It's not fair.
PROUGAULT: I think you have something to celebrate. The inquiry cost you your job, but granted you 90% of your salary. You can sit home, . . . or buy a condo in Mexico.
GALLIARD: I don't deserve this.
PROUGAULT: Sarge nobody would believe that you are guilty. The man who knew most wasn't around. . . . Vanished.

Clarinda watches them from a distance. She waits for Prougault to leave. . . .

Sarge, let the dust settle, and I promise the brotherhood will give you your job. Sarge I have got to go to take care of some business. I will call you.

Prougault exits.

CLARINDA: Galliard, I am really sorry.
GALLIARD: Yeah, thanks.
CLARINDA: But look it's not over yet.
GALLIARD: It is.
CLARINDA: Galliard, there are hundreds of women, who will testify that you are a very good cop.
GALLIARD: Good enough to let go. You know what I have done for them already—Nobody works as . . . . ah shit . . . forget it.
CLARINDA: Wait, . . . no wait . . . Guy. . . .
GALLIARD: Thanks Clarinda, for trying, but I am just a white man.

Lights fade out on them. They leave as Shafiqa, Murad and Shazia come out of the inquiry.

MURAD: Huh, justice?
SHAZIA: It's over.
MURAD: What justice? Making profit out of racism? I wonder whose carpets he is selling?
SHAZIA: Just forget it, let's go.
MURAD: Haramzada. . . .
SHAZIA: Just stop!
MURAD: Do you think a slime ball like him will fight for racial justice without personal benefit?
SHAZIA: I don't want the bloody carpets.
SHAFIQA: I say we sue him. Those carpets belong to her, not Moolchand.

Shazia exits.

MURAD/SHAFIQA: Shazia, wait, Shazia, . . . Shazia. . . .

Meanwhile, on the other side of the stage, Moolchand enters answering questions by off-stage reporters.

MOOLCHAND: Please, one at a time. . . .

Clarinda steps forward, confronts him.

CLARINDA: You were under oath!
MOOLCHAND: I don't have time now, call me. . . .
CLARINDA: Some of us aren't lucky enough to give testimony on behalf of vanished people.
MOOLCHAND: What's your point?
CLARINDA: You lied.
MOOLCHAND: You've got no right to doubt what I said . What did you say in there?
CLARINDA: Do you care about anybody?
MOOLCHAND: Wake up woman. Look what has been accomplished. I think you should be celebrating.
CLARINDA: What do you want me to celebrate? A couple of fucking ethnics on the force? A good cop lost his job. How can I celebrate when no one will take battering seriously!
MOOLCHAND: You had your chance.
CLARINDA: I never had a chance, you make sure of that.
MOOLCHAND: You can always appeal.
CLARINDA: When will Shapoor come out of hiding?
MOOLCHAND: Miss Keith, why don't you hire a detective? And—oh, yes—make sure he is smarter than James Bond.

As lights go out, Clarinda and Moolchand leave in opposite directions. We are back to the present time. Courtroom spotlight appears on Shazia who is under the doorframe located upstage. . . .

SHAZIA: (*In the spotlight*) What? Shapoor called me. Two weeks before sir. No, No! It was the first time I ever went there. Yes. Yes. Sergeant Galliard was there when I got there. No. What? No! I didn't kill him, I loved. . . .

Flashback: lights come up on the house. Murad sits facing the audiences, while Shafiqa stands, looking at the door.

SHAFIQA/MURAD: (*Calling angrily*) Shazia, Shazia!

Shazia walks over from her courtroom spot to the house. Murad shows a letter in his hand.

MURAD: Why didn't you tell us?
SHAZIA: (*Nervous*) What, . . . You opened my letter?
MURAD: Why Shazia?
SHAZIA: Why what?
MURAD: Don't annoy me.
SHAFIQA: You are writing love letters?
MURAD: While everybody thought Moolchand had your lover locked in his basement.
SHAZIA: He's the father of my child.
SHAFIQA: Father? Huh. He is a gunda. A criminal.
MURAD: Where did you find him?
SHAZIA: (*Pauses*) He asked me to let him come to see his child when it's born and I said yes.
SHAFIQA: You're right, She acts like a spoiled maiden in tales.
SHAZIA: Ma, I have made up my mind.
SHAFIQA: You have lost your mind.
MURAD: And you are pig-headed.
SHAZIA: I can't do this! Yes, I wrote the letter, 'cause . . . because . . . I can't bring this baby up alone. How will I support him?
MURAD: You will get those carpets.
SHAZIA: Not now, We can't. Moolchand has them and Shapoor is afraid Moolchand might do something. If we want . . .
SHAFIQA: We?
SHAZIA: Maybe we could . . .
SHAFIQA: We?
SHAZIA: Don't get mad at me, ma.
SHAFIQA: I am not mad, you are.
SHAZIA: You don't understand. . . .
MURAD: No, you don't.
SHAZIA: . . . I miss him.

MURAD: Your beast?

SHAZIA: Don't say that.

MURAD: Yes, your beast. Two hands, two fists, two legs, remember the beast? Last time he left you alive, next time he will bury you. Those charges still stand don't they? I'll call the police. Where is he?

SHAZIA: I dropped the charges.

MURAD: What?

SHAFIQA: Oh, God!

SHAZIA: Look, I know how it sounds, but don't you see? I need him.

MURAD: I would rather be in hell .

SHAFIQA: I have had enough of you girl. If you let that beast come here, I'll kill you. You hear me? I will kill you.

Lights fade out on the family. We are back to the present time. Courtroom spotlight appears on Clarinda who is under the doorframe by her office. . . .

CLARINDA: (*In spotlight*) It really hurt. When I first found out that he had come back, into the city and Shazia had dropped the charges—I just cried. I had to give up. How can you help someone who does not want to be helped? But I did tell her they should get those carpets from Moolchand. Maybe that's what he was trying to do before he got killed.

Flashback: lights come up. We see Shapoor standing on the door and Murad stands facing him. Shazia and Shafiqa stand nearby. There is a long pause before anyone speaks.

SHAFIQA: Murad, let the beast in.

Murad moves away, Shapoor steps in.

SHAPOOR: Hello.

SHAFIQA: (*To Shapoor*) You touch her, and I will kill you. (*To Shazia*) Shazia, your fool is back.

SHAPOOR: (*Smiles*) You look good. Sorry, I thought I knew what I was going to say. (*Looking at her stomach*) I thought you'd be bigger. . . . (*Embarrassed*) That was a stupid thing to say. What's new? . . . You must be so used to my stupid things.

SHAZIA: You are not staying here.

SHAPOOR: No . . . of course not. You had written that to me.

SHAZIA: Then why are you here now? I said after the baby is born. You're lucky my parents haven't killed you.

SHAPOOR: Shazia, I came for one thing. . . .

SHAZIA: I have heard it before.

SHAPOOR: I understand it now. I do. I can't take anything I did away but . . .

SHAZIA: Your father saw you like this, he'd have a heart attack.

SHAPOOR: Shazia . . . my father. . . .

SHAZIA: Is he proud of his son's wife? A machine that pops out babies while the son sells carpets?

SHAPOOR: That is not true.

SHAZIA: Carpet and a wife, . . . they both get walked over.

SHAPOOR: Shazia, please listen to me.

SHAZIA: No, You listen to me. I'll let you see your son but I still have a restraining order and it won't matter what colour the officer is. But don't fool yourself—you will not control this baby like your father controls you.

SHAPOOR: He died. (*Long silence*) I lost him, . . . I lost you.

MURAD: Moolchand is selling your carpets, you fool.

SHAPOOR: I know, I'm taking care of the carpets. Shazia, look, (*He pulls out some document*) I've started therapy. My counsellor says I'm not a wife beater.

MURAD: Oh! How come she's a battered wife?

SHAPOOR: I am learning to control my temper. I am doing everything I can to correct myself. You know, I even meditate. Can you forgive me? I need to know if you can—if there is hope, any hope . . . that you could forgive . . .

SHAZIA: I haven't forgotten anything.

SHAPOOR: Please . . . give me a chance . . . one last time. Not now, at this minute. But maybe in time. . . .

SHAZIA: Shapoor, I'm very scared.

SHAPOOR: Maybe you'll need me. I'll be the baby sitter. I'll do things other Iranian men don't do. I'll cook, I'll clean. . . .

MURAD: . . . And call cops racist.

SHAPOOR: That was Moolchand, I'm sorry about that. I called that officer, Galliard. I'm seeing him tomorrow to see if there is anything I can do.

SHAZIA: I am afraid.

SHAPOOR: I know. Me too. Here is my number at the "Y." I won't call you again until you want me to. When you are ready. I will wait.

He pulls out his address card, Murad takes it.

SHAZIA: Shapoor. . . . Come tomorrow.

SHAPOOR: No, You think about it. Good bye Shazia.

Shapoor exits.

SHAZIA: Ummi. . . .

Shafiqa does not answer. Shazia exits. Shafiqa takes the address card from Murad. Lights narrow on her as she dials the police station.

SHAFIQA: (*On the phone*) Hello, officer Prougault please. . . . Hello sir. Begum Shafiqa Rizvi here. Shazia's mother. Good. The carpet seller is back in town. . . . I thought he was her ex, but he is trying hard to become her present. . . . Help me sir, I know she said she made a mistake. But there must be something you can do. Yes, yes, he was just here, he left a number. . . .

Lights fade out on the family as we return back to the present time. Courtroom spotlight appears on Murad who has walked over to the doorframe on the other side of the stage.

MURAD: (*In spotlight*) That's all she did. Just gave the police his number. No that was the last time we saw him. Yes the last time I saw him. Yes. Yes. . . .

Courtroom spotlight shifts from Murad to Moolchand. . . .

MOOLCHAND: (*In spotlight*) Well someone must have them then, I swear I don't. No he had those papers, I threw them on the bed. Yes. In that YMCA room. And he was very much alive.

Flashback: lights come up on YMCA room where Shapoor was staying. By changing the bed covers, the family bed is now being represented as the YMCA room. Moolchand enters with a file full of papers. . . .

MOOLCHAND: This is it. All I ever will have to do with you again. . . (*Holds the papers*) They are in your wife's name.

SHAPOOR: You lied.

MOOLCHAND : What?

SHAPOOR: You lied in the inquiry. I never said those things. I wanted to drop . . .

MOOLCHAND: I don't care what you think. Here, . . . you wanted your carpets, here are the papers. Sorry they do not come back 100%. I had expenses in trying to save your sorryful head. Now good bye and please never call me again.

Moolchand throws papers on the bed, starts to go to the door.

SHAPOOR: Why did you lie?

MOOLCHAND: You want to undo everything I did?

SHAPOOR: I wanted to drop those charges against Galliard. Why did . . .

MOOLCHAND: You fucking wife beater, you broke the restraining order, you beat the hell out of her. You ask me why?

SHAPOOR: I told you to drop those . . .

MOOLCHAND: We finally have some coloured cops on the force to help people like you. Do you want to know what I said in the inquiry? What they did not want to hear! Should I have waited for you to come back? I didn't need you any more, I had better witnesses against that cop. You don't get it, do you? What would have happened if I lost the inquiry? Revenge from the cops! More racism! People would have laughed at us. No ethnic would have dared talk about racial justice in this city. Drop the charges. . . . Fuck you!

Moolchand leaves. Shapoor runs to the door . . .

SHAPOOR: Pedah sahg! You used me. What I did to my wife was wrong. I was wrong. But you manipulated me. You turned my crime against my wife into a crime against the colour of our bloody skin. You abused us. You wanted to win, . . . it didn't matter about anybody else, did it? Well, you won you bastard. You're a big shot today. What about me? How do I get back my wife?

Lights fade out on Shapoor. We are back to the present time. Courtroom spotlight appears on Moolchand who is now standing under the doorframe near Clarinda's office.

MOOLCHAND: (*In spotlight*) Then I left. I swear he was holding them. What would I gain? The carpets were in his wife's name. I mean why would I care what happened to him. He had lost his life the moment he hit that woman.

Spotlight out on Moolchand. Courtroom spotlight appears on Shazia who is now near Clarinda's office.

SHAZIA: (*In spotlight*) I keep thinking if only I got there, even 10 minutes earlier. I know he . . . he did things to me. But he didn't deserve to die. If only I got there before Sgt Galliard . . .

Flashback: lights come up to the YMCA room again. Shapoor is on the phone. As he puts down the phone, Prougault enters. Shapoor surprised. . . .

SHAPOOR: Oh, ah . . . Hi, sir, is there something wrong?

PROUGAULT: You seemed surprised.

SHAPOOR: Yes, I was expecting Galliard, I just called him. I just wanted to tell him . . .

PROUGAULT: Why do you need to talk with him? Haven't you destroyed his life enough already.

SHAPOOR: No, no, Moolchand said those things, see that's why I need to talk.

PROUGAULT: Quiet, I thought we had an understanding?

SHAPOOR: I know we did, I know. I just wanted to apologize to him. I thought it wouldn't matter if I came back now.

PROUGAULT: Don't you think that might be little dangerous?

SHAPOOR: What? Why?

PROUGAULT: What are you going to do? Clear his name?

SHAPOOR: Well, no. But if I could . . .

PROUGAULT: You want to reopen the inquiry?

SHAPOOR: No, I just want to say sorry to him.

PROUGAULT: I smell a plot.

SHAPOOR: What? You have no reason.

PROUGAULT: What's the last thing you said to me. You forgot that? You want me to remind you?

Lights go out on them. Courtroom spotlight appears on Galliard who is standing under the upstage doorframe.

GALLIARD: (*In spotlight*) (*Very nervous*) When? The second time he was arrested? What? It was—I don't know ah, . . . When Shapoor . . . It was just before he took the plane back to India. What? I . . . uh, I don't. . . . Alright . . . Alright! (*Pause*) Prougault had him in this room, I just happened in. I overheard them. . . . It wasn't my idea. I was actually . . .

Flashback: lights come up on the detention cell. The audiences should see Shapoor and Moolchand as they were seen in the detention cell when Shapoor was brought in after breaking the restraining order and attacking Shazia. Following part of that scene is repeated exactly like before . . .

SHAPOOR: (*Whispers*) Please help me, . . . Please get me out of here. I promise I will not come back. Sell all those damn carpets if you. . . .

PROUGAULT: (*Off-stage*) Time's up.

MOOLCHAND: Shh . . . Don't speak with anyone until I come back.

SHAPOOR: Don't go, . . . No

SHAPOOR: (*Hugging Moolchand's knees*) Don't go, . . . No, . . . Please.

MOOLCHAND: I will be back soon,
PROUGAULT: Time's up mister.
MOOLCHAND: Come on stand up. (*In Prougault's direction*) Yes, Thank you sir, thank you.

Moolchand hugs Shapoor, whispers something secretly in his ear like before and exits. Prougault enters.

PROUGAULT: (*To Shapoor*) If 100 thousand French Canadians landed in India, what do you think would happen?
PROUGAULT: They'd screw up the country?
SHAPOOR: I don't know.
PROUGAULT: Here we have 100 thousand Moolchands in Quebec. And what do you think they're doing?
SHAPOOR: I am sorry sir, I don't know!
PROUGAULT: I think you do. get up.

Shapoor extends his arms to be handcuffed.

I'm not putting any handcuffs on you. No, not there . . . that door.

Repeat of the scene ends.
Now we see the remainder of the scene as the flashback continues. We see Prougault bringing Shapoor into another interrogation room, seats him down on a stool. He puts his foot on the stool Shapoor is sitting and leans over to Shapoor . . .

PROUGAULT: So I heard you planning a little escape? Yeah, the walls are paper thin. I can't believe you were talking about leaving without an apology.
SHAPOOR: I wasn't planning.
PROUGAULT: No, no. Don't say anything . . . remember what your friend said? You know . . . I'm hurt.
SHAPOOR: Sir, listen. . . .
PROUGAULT: No Please don't say anything now. It's too late for apologies. I just can't believe an Iranian, . . . I said that right, didn't I? An Iranian, and an Indian, are holding us ransom.
SHAPOOR: Please sir, I'm not . . .

Meanwhile, Galliard has walked up to the door. He stands there without being noticed by Prougault and Shapoor. He listens in on what Prougault is telling Shapoor.

PROUGAULT: Shh. . . . He said don't talk. You beat your wife didn't you? (*Shapoor nods*) Is that fair? You assaulted a woman and I have to treat you better than the Prime Minister? Bad example eh? And now . . . this inquiry . . . what do you think will happen if I don't get re-elected? This inquiry is causing me concern. Or maybe it doesn't matter. Maybe we should elect an Iranian as the president of the Brotherhood. You guys can't even run your own fucking country right, . . . Damn I am mad. I got all these problems. Why? Why? I know, I know. (*Directly at Shapoor*) You drop all your racial charges against us.

SHAPOOR: I tried. I will, but Mr. Moolchand, he . . . oh please, my father is in jail in India, he's dying, . . . Please sir, let me go there. I will never come back here, promise.

PROUGAULT: Moolchand wouldn't have much of an inquiry without you, would he?

SHAPOOR: No sir, . . . I beg you. Just let me out. I just need some money. I can take the next plane . . .

PROUGAULT: Who . . . hold the camel, we have rules here. What'd you think — I just open the door and out you go?

Prougault turns around. Notices that Galliard was listening to him.

Oh hello Guy,—doing a little eavesdropping? . . . Hey, maybe you can escort our friend here to the airport.

GALLIARD: What?

PROUGAULT: We've got to get him out of the country before the inquiry.

GALLIARD: Sir he can't go, there's no bond.

PROUGAULT: You want your fucking job back?

GALLIARD: But . . . It's not legal.

PROUGAULT: We'll let him out on a stricter restraining order.

SHAPOOR: You let me go, I will keep my mouth shut. I promise. Nobody will know anything. Even Mr. Moolchand won't know what . . .

GALLIARD: This isn't right.

PROUGAULT: We'll make it right.

GALLIARD: I don't know about this.

SHAPOOR: I promise.

PROUGAULT: This might save both our asses.

GALLIARD: Sir, . . . you can't.

SHAPOOR: Sir, thank you sir, thank you. . . .

PROUGAULT: Shut up, you can both count yourselves lucky. Now Galliard take him to the airport, I'll book the flight.

Lights fade out on them. Prougault leaves stage as we come back to the present time.Courtroom spotlights appear on Galliard who is now moved under the centre stage doorframe. . . .

GALLIARD: (*In spotlight*) That's what he said,—"I'll book the flight." No. I didn't know. I did it because I wanted my job back. He was the one that was afraid Shapoor would talk.

PROUGAULT: (*In dark*) That's a lie. You're a Goddamn liar. Whose name was on the purchase of the tickets.

GALLIARD: (*In spotlight*) Yeah, I put it on my Visa. He was supposed to pay me back. He said . . .

PROUGAULT: (*In dark*) I am not on trial here. You are. You're the one.

Meanwhile Moolchand, dressed in tuxedo and bow tie, stands under the doorframe by Clarinda's office. As lights brighten, he delivers a speech to an imaginary crowd.

MOOLCHAND: Thank you for the honour of the Indo-Canadian of the year. Thank you. Honourable guest, friends, and dear community leaders, Canada is the best country in the world and it couldn't be the best without us making it best. . . .

Lights cross fade from Moolchand to YMCA room where Prougault was talking to Shapoor. . . .

PROUGAULT: I think I'm going to have to put you back on the plane again.

SHAPOOR: You can't.

PROUGAULT: Can't I?

SHAPOOR: Please officer, I will keep my mouth shut about what happened. I promise. I won't tell anyone anything.

PROUGAULT: Why should I believe you? Didn't you already break your promise by coming back?

SHAPOOR: Look, I don't want any trouble with the police.

Prougault moves towards Shapoor who steps back.

SHAPOOR: Here, take my carpets, please I will not say anything to anyone. Please!

Lights cross fade from YMCA room back to Moolchand who continues his speech.

MOOLCHAND: . . . Some years ago, I was already a Canadian citizen, had a degree from McGill and one from New Delhi and an immigrant's discipline. But I was bumped out of a job. Why? ". .

Mr. Moolchand belongs to a behind-the-desk job—at the census bureau, for example, where many of his countrymen are doing wonderful work." . . .

As Moolchand continues his speech, dim lights fade in on YMCA room. We see Shapoor lying on the bed as in the opening scene. Prougault looks around and exits the room. Galliard enters like he had come to the YMCA room like in the opening scene, . . . As Moolchand continues with his speech, the audience see the opening scene being repeated in front of their eyes in dim light and low volume. Meanwhile Moolchand continues his delivery. . . .

MOOLCHAND: . . . "He is not a suitable candidate for the classroom." I guess it was my Bombaywallah accent and my lack of humour. Do you think I lack humour? The reason was, They will let you get only so far ahead and then they will cut you down. And we still need more coloured police on the force. Let's not forget, the man shouldn't have hit his wife, and I didn't know the answer to his problem! But that didn't give a police officer the right to bully him, racially. It is as simple as that. I still don't feel safe in their company. If my car stops at a red light and I see a cop car, I want him to notice that I have broken *no* law because I know the cops are in the habit of prejudging us as law violators. Anthony Griffin was prejudged as a shoplifter. Albert Johnson prejudged as a murderer. Marcelles Françoise, . . . as a drug dealer. Barnabe as a lunatic. And the list goes on. The result is always the same—we lose our citizenship or we lose our lives, . . . always in "self-defence," . . .'n always a case of "mistaken identity." But I promise you that with your support, no Shapoor will have to leave the country, and no Farhadi will lose his life! That is why we want a strong voice for racial justice.

Gradually lights go out on the YMCA. Then the lights circle on Moolchand and slowly begin to narrow on him until entire stage goes in complete darkness.